The Life of Worship:
Rethink, Reform, Renew

The Life of Worship: Rethink, Reform, Renew

Mark S. Sooy

Published by Blue Maroon

The Life of Worship: Rethink, Reform, Renew
Mark S. Sooy

Copyright © 2006 Mark Scot Sooy

ISBN-10: 1-60145-047-8
ISBN-13: 978-1-60145-047-0

Printed in the United States of America.

Scripture quotations taken from the
New American Standard Bible®,
Copyright © 1960, 1962, 1963, 1968, 1971, 1972, 1973,
1975, 1977, 1995 by The Lockman Foundation.
Used by permission. (www.Lockman.org)

For clarity, all Scripture quoted within the text will be found in regular *italics*.
Author's points of emphasis are in ***bold italics.***

Published by Blue Maroon
in cooperation with Booklocker.com, Inc.

For more information about this book, the author, or other available
resources visit www.blue-maroon.com.

For the men, women and children
of New Song Ministries
who exemplified a true life of worship.

Contents

Acknowledgments

There are many people who have been part of the process in developing the ideas in these pages. Over the years I have taught these concepts in sermons, Sunday Schools, classrooms, small group Bible studies and other venues. The questions and comments of the hearers have helped to clarify much of what is written. Thank you.

More directly, I would also like to thank those who were willing to read through the rough drafts and make comments, corrections and suggestions to be sure I was communicating clearly and succinctly. Thanks must go to Bruce Hoeker, Aimee Johnson, Scott Merriner, Bob Stauffer, Dr. Michael Wittmer, Cliff Wheeler and Elisabeth Sooy for giving their time and energy in this way.

Great thanks to my brother, Brian Sooy, whose expertise in graphic design continues to amaze me. Thanks for fitting in these projects in the midst of your other work! By the way, visit Brian and his company at www.briansooyco.com.

I am truly grateful for my own family. Elisabeth, my wife, and our children: Estelle, Ashlea and Gordon. You have been patient, supportive and then patient some more. Thank you for believing in this as much as I do.

And to our Lord: I thank You for all of these people and the rich grace You have shown me in my own life of worship.

Part I: A Foundation for Worship

Several years ago my wife and I bought some land. It was a beautiful piece of property with enormous trees and a creek winding gently through the lower half of the yard. The raised part of the land was the place for our house and we had to clear trees and shrubs, dig out stumps, and generally make room for the machinery to come in and work.

It was not too long before a large backhoe was busy digging a massive hole. The hole was deep and level at the bottom so the concrete trucks could follow and add their piece to the puzzle. As the concrete pump truck extended its long arm, it released the liquid concrete mixture into the forms that had been placed to create the walls of the basement, as well as other sections of the underlying foundation. It was an impressive sight.

Not many days later workers removed the forms to reveal the basement walls. The walls were thick and hard, and ready to supply stability for the house that would rest upon them. Because we were building on the side of a hill, we built a wooden frame wall for the "walk-out" side of the basement facing the creek in the lower part of the property. Basically, the basement consisted of three concrete walls, and a wooden wall with windows and a door. Eventually, the house was placed on top of the basement that had been prepared for it.

Now that we have lived here a while, one can hardly imagine those first few months of construction. The holes are filled in, the grass is mature, and the landscaping is in place. Dirt covers most of the concrete, and siding is installed on the "walk-out" side of the basement. Generally speaking, the foundation of the house is almost completely covered. Unless you witnessed the original work, it would be difficult to know how deep and how thick the foundation really is. In a sense, the foundation is invisible. So is the framework of the house, now covered with siding on the exterior and drywall on the interior.

I would suspect that the "hidden" foundation and framework of our house is true for most who live in a home. We know it is there, and trust it to be secure and safe, but we do not necessarily see it now that the whole structure is complete. And though almost invisible, it is absolutely essential for the usefulness and the safety of the dwelling. The foundation and framework is what provides stability. Without the foundation the building would be uncertain. Without the frame it would crumble. It would be unable to function as intended.

Although it is often unseen, the foundation and framework is vital to the existence and proper functioning of any building. The ideas presented in this book are meant to be like that. In my mind's eye, I see it as providing a framework for something larger than itself, yet completely dependent upon it. A foundation that will support and provide stability yet be often invisible to the thing itself. It must be adaptable and flexible to support great variety, yet give a solid structure to hold and anchor the various methods and participants.

Of course, the frame I wish to build is a framework for worship. Not necessarily a bunch of "how-to" methods, though there is plenty of "how-to" included in these pages, but *an underlying foundation and framework within which worship can be conceived and practiced in a variety of settings.*[1] It is meant to be a broad consideration of the foundational, supporting thought behind a well-rounded view of worship. It is to be foundational so that it can support the many shapes and sizes and methods that will be built upon it.

Worldview

To employ the popular language of one strain of Christian thought, this book can be considered a "worldview" for worship. Michael Wittmer, in his introductory book on the subject of worldview, notes that a common theme running through various definitions of the term "worldview" suggests, "A worldview is a framework of fundamental concepts or beliefs about the world. In short, a worldview comprises the lens through which we see the world."[2] This book, using these terms, is meant to be a "lens" through which we can view worship—its thought and form and practice—within a biblical framework and an overall Christian worldview.

Because I am writing with this broad concept in mind, my comments will be a "framework of fundamental concepts or beliefs" about worship. I believe that many of the problems experienced in the corporate activity generally referred to as "worship" could be avoided if the right thinking was underneath (providing a solid frame for) the practice of worship. The struggle and misunderstanding in congregations worldwide tell us that the turmoil is one of ideas, not simply disagreement over methods.

Admittedly, the framework I seek to build is limited, in this sense: it concerns the Christian God. The God found in Trinity—Father, Son and Holy Spirit. The God extolled in the sixty-six books of the Bible. The God of Abraham, Isaac and Jacob. The God of Paul, Silas and Peter. The God of Augustine, Luther and Calvin. The God of the Apostles' Creed and the great Catechisms. We find in Scripture no other focus and no other god for the proper object of our worship.

Yet, I also intend for this framework to be so flexible that it allows limitless possibilities for the expression of worship. Different styles, sizes and speeds. Various cultural and

3

ideological idiosyncrasies. Open arms for the arts and creativity. An unending display of God's people thankfully acknowledging all that God has done, and is doing, in and among them. I hope for worship that explodes with variety and fervor limited only by the imagination and energy of those that are worshiping.

In many ways, and in many churches, the Body of Christ is stuck. Trapped in a pit of confusion and mired in the mud of methodology. We have supposedly been taught the right **methods, styles** and **forms** of worship but have either not been instructed in, or have not listened to, the right way to **think** about worship. We have not learned the foundation, as I mentioned above, to build our practice of worship upon. When the foundation is unstable, anything built upon it is unstable as well. The need for reform in our theology of worship continues in the footsteps of the Reformation, which began so many years ago.

Reform for Worship

When we think back to the Reformation of the Church in the 16th Century, we find the great Reformers critiquing the established Roman Catholic Church and seeking reform of its practice of worship, its relationship with government, its domination of the common people, and its morals. What we do not often understand is the underlying issues that generated these calls for change and renewal.

The basis for reform during the Reformation was theology. The Reformers knew, for example, that changing the morality of the church, without renewing its theology, would be no reform at all. This point comes through in various writings, and is quite apparent in Martin Luther's discussion and correspondence with Didymus Erasmus.

Erasmus was a devout Catholic, and the greatest proponent of the Humanist movement (The *Humanists* in the 16th Century, unlike the way we apply the term today, were devoted specifically to the cultivation and study of classical literature and they extended this renewal into the areas of philosophy and theology as well). Erasmus saw the abuses of the Roman Church and desired reform. Early on, he agreed with Luther's calls for reform, but eventually broke with Luther rather than leaving the Roman Church. In the ensuing discussion with Luther,[3] it is apparent that ***Erasmus saw the need for reform on primarily moral grounds***. In other words, Erasmus argued, if the church could reform the way it lived (especially by correcting the abuses of the papacy), it could then return to its roots and be the light needed in a dark world.

Luther, on the other hand, took on Erasmus (and the Roman Church) by challenging and ***seeking reform in the underlying theology of the church***. This theology, in Luther's view, led to both corruption of its practices, and oppression of the people. His point was that true reform was to begin with a clear understanding of theology and doctrine—especially as found in Scripture. After the Bible, the study of the great Creeds of the ancient church (Apostles' Creed, Nicene Creed and Athanasius Creed) were to be a guide to the church for the understanding of God and theology. Beyond that, the writings of the ancient fathers themselves were to be consulted. All of these sources of theology, however, must adhere to the clear teachings of Scripture. No creed, council, or pope could override the teaching of the Bible. Roland Bainton, in his classic treatment of Luther's life, summarizes, "The craving of Erasmus to confine himself to the clear and simple (i.e., moralistic reforms) spelled for Luther the abandonment of Christianity, for the reason that Christianity cannot be simple and obvious to the natural man."[4]

It was from this foundation of clearly defined biblical theology that Luther then would call for other reforms in the

5

Christian life and practice. And that he did. His wide-reaching commentary on, and reform of, the life of the church was astounding, as well as his commentary, critique and improvements for political life and family life. We are the heirs of his reforms, as were the other Reformers who came in his wake or sought changes in other geographical areas.

It is in this spirit that we, today, must continue to seek reform of our own churches. The need is clear in the world of worship theories and methods that abound in the modern Evangelical church. Although there has been a great deal of discussion in the area of corporate worship, only in a consistent re-thinking, reform and renewal of our theology of worship, based upon Scripture (and those traditions in agreement with Scripture), can our practice of worship, both individually and corporately, become honoring to God and be in keeping with His desires.

Actions Flow from Beliefs

Scripture regularly points out that our **actions** are the result of our **thinking**. More specifically—right actions result from correct thinking (1 Peter 1:13-16; Eph 4:20-24; 1 John 2:3-6; and others). Over and over again we are told to *"prepare your minds for action,"* (1 Peter 1:13), or to *"be renewed in the spirit of your mind"* (Ephesians 4:23), or to be *"transformed by the renewing of your mind"* (Romans 12:2).

Should we wonder that these same admonitions also apply to our worship? We all have heard horror stories about church splits as a result of changes in worship methods and styles. The tales of "worship wars," in which opposing sides battle to place their preferred style of worship as pre-eminent over other styles, are only too familiar within the last twenty or more years. The striking truth of the matter is that much of this upheaval has little to do with worship style, although that is where the battle seems to rage. In reality, the underlying issue in these "worship wars" is a shortsighted and shallow philosophical and theological understanding about worship itself. Unfortunately, this shortage of insight resides in both the leadership and the laity.

If the right belief system can be established concerning worship, then extremes that cause divisions might possibly be avoided. As mentioned earlier, our thinking will direct and determine our actions. Thus, *correct thinking about worship will guide our practice of worship*. This will include a solid, broadly defined theological understanding of worship based upon Scripture. Our Scriptural and theological understanding will, in turn, lead to the transformation of our daily Christian walk. It will also include a realignment of some forms or patterns of corporate worship. Finally, it will allow for a complete experience of worship in all of its joy, sorrow and other emotions.

Theological Foundation

Recognizing the importance of our thinking is essentially a call for theological renewal. This theological renewal is at the heart of how we think about worship and is much broader than simply doing a study on worship as it is found in various Biblical texts. Our theology of worship must be based upon a holistic understanding and foundation of what God meant for our relationship with Him. What it was like at the beginning, what happened that distorted it so grossly, and what He has done to restore (redeem) us to Himself. This pattern of thought—creation, fall, and redemption—is the classic pattern used in discussing worldview systems. Ultimately, our theology of worship unfolds out of our own worldview. Only in this broad-based picture can we truly develop theology which is both consistent with Scripture and tradition, yet adapts itself to our modern times and situations.

It is, therefore, imperative that we seek to mold our view of worship to one that is grounded in Scripture. We must seek renewal, not based upon new methods and theories, but by renewing our minds and hearts based on a study of God's word. It is time to redeem worship theory and practice and return to foundational truths that transverse denominations, styles and cultures. It is, in short, time for reform.

A.W. Tozer said it pointedly:

> Every spiritual problem is at bottom theological. Its solution will depend upon the teaching of the Holy Scriptures plus a correct understanding of that teaching. That correct understanding constitutes a spiritual philosophy, that is, a viewpoint, a high vantage ground from which the whole landscape may be seen at once, each detail appearing in its proper relation to everyone else. Once such a vantage ground is gained, we are in a position to evaluate any teaching or interpretation that is offered us in the name of truth.[5]

Tozer's words continue to speak to the heart of what ails many churches today in the area of worship—theologically, philosophically and methodologically. There is no shortage of opinions out there floating through cyber-space, and in print, that fall short of recognizing the foundational theological issues that face our churches in the area of worship.

I hope that this book will be both the beginning of, and the continuation of, the discussion of worship theology. By saying this, I wish to recognize and appreciate the many men and women who have gone before me studying, struggling, practicing and writing on this subject—from whom I have studied, struggled, practiced and written. I also realize that my treatment of the subject of worship might be somewhat atypical in comparison to other studies.

There has been a lot of good work done in the last thirty years in the study and advancement of worship as a discipline and activity of the church. As I review the books on my shelf, and think through the various lines of discussion in current circles, it seems that much of what has been written deals with methodology. Whether it is revival and renewal in liturgical worship, focus and organization in "free" worship, or a combination of the two, the propensity of topics deals with the practical aspects of the public worship service, or corporate worship. Most often, the focus is on music—what is right, what is wrong, why we are right, why they are wrong, etc.

What I have not found in my reading and study is more than a few authors dealing with what I perceive as the heart of the matter, that is, what I would call a "theology of worship." As you read on, you will begin to understand why I feel this is so important, and why my discussion of worship will take unusual turns from the common patterns associated with this topic. I hope it will both encourage and challenge you to think further and deeper in regards to worship.

Please read with a heart of prayer, curiosity to explore further, a mind ready to stretch and grow, and a whole life desirous and willing to honor God in all that you do. In this journey I will gladly join you.

The Starting Point

Romans 12:1-2 is a significant and foundational passage on the subject of worship. This passage could very well be the heart and soul of worship theology—and practice—but it is often overlooked or disregarded. In the books on worship found on my library shelves, I have located only a few references to the passage, and even less definitive commentary on it in regards to our worship. I am not sure why this is the case and would like to begin to remedy this situation, especially because we consider ourselves to be Christian people desiring to model Christianity based upon the New Testament.

I would like to present the concepts found here as *primary* for the foundation which should support our entire perceptual framework concerning worship. Not only is this the starting point, but we also must consider it the corner stone of the structure itself. The ideas Paul presents in Romans 12 establish the characteristics of both personal and corporate worship. Using this passage as a jumping point for all other developments of worship theology gives us a solid foundation on which to build. It also provides a reference for balancing all of the facets of worship into a unified whole.

Let me clarify right at the outset that the word "worship" has been so overused and ill defined that its definition today has become muddled. That being said, it remains an excellent word for the topic under consideration because it is the Biblical word. You will notice, however, that I will often qualify the word worship by the use of "personal" or "corporate." In a broader sense I will use the phrases "life of worship" or "worship as a lifestyle" or something similar to indicate the breadth of ideas presented in Scripture. This idea of a "lifestyle of worship" includes the more limited and popular approach to discussing worship—that of the worship service, or corporate worship—but includes it **only as a portion** of the overall concept and life of worship itself. As you read, be sure to pay close attention to the differences in meanings of these qualifiers and which of these I am discussing. What I am attempting to build is an idea of worship as a lifestyle in which personal worship and corporate worship are two parts of a larger whole. Corporate worship, in fact, being the smaller of the two.

Romans 12:1-2

I urge you therefore, brethren, by the mercies of God, to present your bodies a living and holy sacrifice, acceptable to God, which is your spiritual service of worship. And do not be conformed to this world, but be transformed by the renewing of your mind, that you may prove what the will of God is, that which is good and acceptable and perfect. (Romans 12:1-2)

Note that Paul begins this statement based upon God's mercy. If you were to back up a few verses to the end of Romans 11, you would find several verses exalting in the greatness of Who God is and what He has done. *"Oh, the depth of the riches both of the wisdom and knowledge of God!"* Paul writes, *"How unsearchable are His judgments and unfathomable His ways!"* (Romans 11:33) It is God's mercy and love, toward us who do not deserve it, which allow us to present ourselves to Him in worship. One commentator notes that these verses bridge a gap in our understanding:

...the chasm that always exists, at least potentially, between doctrine and living. Mere acquaintance with "the mercies of God" does not create for the Christian the ability to discern, embrace, and verify God's will in daily affairs, for this knowledge becomes effective only when its yokefellows are total dedication and daily growth. Conversely, a desire to live according to God's will gains power and relevance only when grounded in "the mercies" and the commitment appropriate to them.[6]

Without the work of God—through Christ upon the cross—our attempts at associating with, living for, or worshiping God would be futile. It is His movement toward us (not us toward Him) that establishes the relationship between God and man. This is one of the main emphases of the entire book of Romans, and Paul tells us that we "*fall short*" of drawing ourselves toward Him and that we consistently seek everything other than God. Romans 3:9-11 says that "*both Jews and Greeks are all under sin; as it is written, 'There is none righteous, not even one; There is none who understands, there is none who seeks for God.*'" When Paul uses the phrase "*Jews and Greeks*" he is not referring only to those nationalities, but in a broad reference to all people of every nationality.

Let us always remember this: it is God that moves toward us in mercy, and we respond by His mercy. Both His mercy toward us and our response to Him are His gifts to us. Not only is this the message of Romans, it is also encapsulated in Ephesians 2:8-10,

> *For by grace you have been saved through faith; and that not of yourselves, it is the gift of God; not as a result of works, that no one should boast. For we are His workmanship, created in Christ Jesus for*

> *good works, which God prepared beforehand, that we*
> *should walk in them.*

If we keep this point at the core of our discussion we will recognize His gift of salvation through the cross of Christ, and His ongoing work in us through the presence of the Holy Spirit.

Paul continues in Romans 12 by telling us to *"present your bodies a living and holy sacrifice, acceptable to God."* Our faith is more than a faith of intellectual assent. We are not believers if we only agree to the **propositions** of the faith, and do not also conform our **actions** to a life of faith. There must be an external representation of our internal convictions. James is clear in emphasizing this point as well when he writes, *"Even so faith, if it has no works, is dead, being by itself"* (James 2:17; see also James 2:14-26 for the complete context). James rightly says that we cannot show our faith without works, for works are the externalizing of our faith. These works come **after** our salvation, as a result of our faith. Our salvation is holistic, encompassing body, mind, and soul.

Combating Dualism

In this way Paul is dismantling a certain dualism in our culture and thought that may creep into our life of worship. (Dualism, in simplistic form, is a belief that the "inner" or spiritual part of man is good, and that the "outer" or physical part is evil.) He tells us to present our **bodies** as a **spiritual service**, mixing the spiritual and the physical. Have you ever wondered why he does not advise prayer, or Bible reading, or any other internal "spiritual discipline" as what we should present to God in worship? Western Christians seem to understand the "spiritual disciplines" (i.e., Bible reading, prayer, meditation, fasting, worship, etc.)

as those elements of our faith that are internal by nature, rather than physical. It is in this philosophy of the Christian life that we see a dualism glaringly apparent in our Christian walk. Many believe that the internal or "spiritual" things we do are more presentable, holy, or worshipful to God and the physical aspects of life are considered less honorable, and not necessarily spiritual by nature.

This dualistic view of life has caused a rupture in the very core of what Paul refers to as a *"spiritual service of worship."* It is only in a unified, holistic approach that worship can be understood correctly. ***Presenting our bodies is spiritual by nature and acceptable to God as worship.*** As Nancy Pearcey notes,

> It is only when we offer up everything we do in worship to God that we finally experience His power coursing through every fiber of our being. The God of the Bible is not only the God of the human spirit but also the God of nature and history. We serve Him not only in worship but also in obedience to the Cultural Mandate. If Christian churches are serious about discipleship, they must teach believers how to keep living for God after they walk out the church doors on Sunday.[7]

Paul moves on to juxtapose the offering of our body in worship with an essential non-conformity with the world and its supposed "pleasures," which are often bodily in nature. The "world" being spoken of is not the "earth" or the many God-given pleasures we enjoy in creation and within relationships with others, but "world" refers to the system, or culture, of the world enslaved to Satan and turning away from God. John in his first epistle notes the general breadth of this:

> *Do not love the world, nor the things of the world.*
> *If anyone loves the world, the love of the Father is not*
> *in him. For all that is in the world, the lust of the flesh,*
> *the lust of the eyes and the boastful pride of life, is not*
> *from the Father, but is from the world.* (1 John 2:15-
> 16)

Paul actually gets very specific in Galatians 5:16-21 by listing the *"deeds of the flesh"* which describe the worldly lusts and desires (a life "conformed" to the world):

> *Now the deeds of the flesh are evident, which are:*
> *immorality, impurity, sensuality, idolatry, sorcery,*
> *enmities, strife, jealousy, outbursts of anger, disputes,*
> *dissensions,   factions,   envying,   drunkenness,*
> *carousing, and things like these, of which I forewarn*
> *you just as I have forewarned you that those who*
> *practice such things shall not inherit the kingdom of*
> *God.*

And then he lists the *"fruit of the Spirit"* in Galatians 5:22-24, which describes a life *"not conformed"* to the world:

> *But the fruit of the Spirit is love, joy, peace,*
> *patience, kindness, goodness, faithfulness, gentleness,*
> *self-control; against such things there is no law. Now*
> *those who belong to Christ Jesus have crucified the*
> *flesh with its passions and desires.*

These verses are the meat on the bones, so to speak, of the phrases we find in John's epistle, as well as in Romans 12:1-2.

Balancing Mind and Body

Next, Paul balances the idea of presenting our physical **bodies** with the idea of presenting our **minds** to God (Romans 12:2). Once again, our actions of worship (i.e., our lifestyle of worship) are inseparable from our thoughts and beliefs about worship. As Horrace Stoessel so succinctly points out,

> The aspect of Paul's use of [mind] which reveals the nature of the "common mind" in Romans 12:2 is the *objective* aspect, by which is meant that [mind] always includes the idea of an external standard. Sometimes "standard" is the primary idea; in these passages [mind] is virtually equivalent to "theology," that is, the ideas or principles which are the springs of action.[8]

As God's word transforms our minds (in all of its facets) individually and as a community, we are able to "prove" or "discern" what the will of God is. As quoted above, we understand "the ideas or principles which are the springs of action." In other words, we will know more readily how to present our bodies as a *"spiritual service of worship"* when we understand more intimately the character of God and His desires for us as revealed in Scripture.

Note how Paul intertwines the working of the mind with the actions of the body by drawing on parallel terms in *"living and holy sacrifice, acceptable to God,"* and *"that which is good and acceptable and perfect."* Our mind is internal, our bodies are external, and we as people live in both realms. Since our actions flow from our inner thoughts, we must make it a serious matter to "renew" our minds to conform to God's character and desires for our life. This is the life of worship.

Francis Schaeffer, founder of *L'Abri Fellowship* and an influential mid-20th Century Christian thinker, makes a similar point in reference to the overall Christian life—what I am calling *the life of worship*. He states it in this way,

> So here we move on in our understanding of true spirituality in the Christian life. Basically it is a matter of our *thoughts*. The external is the expression, the result. Moral battles are not won in the external world first. They are always a result flowing naturally from the cause, and the cause is the internal world of one's thoughts.[9]

Schaeffer shows that the pattern is always the same: thought first, then action. Here in Romans 12, Paul is using this same pattern. It is not enough for us to only give assent to the right knowledge (doctrine), nor is it enough to merely act in the right way (worship methods). Our practice of worship must flow from a solid theological and biblical foundation.

I appreciate the way Stoessel summarizes by saying that Paul "refers to a process embracing two distinct though not independent steps: (1) receiving and affirming a basic theology; (2) discerning and acknowledging the implications of that theology for my personal situation."[10] Here we find our pattern for a framework and foundation for worship. Worship is revealed as a complete life that honors God, whether individually in our daily lives or corporately in our worship together.

Our worship (the presentation of our bodies) should flow naturally from the cause (our thinking/worldview of worship). It is not enough to do the actions. It is not enough to think the correct thoughts. *Our activity of worship—both individually and corporately—must derive from correct and biblical thinking about worship, and then flow out into activities that are offered to God as worship.* When you set this as the foundational principle of worship, as I hope this book will help you to do, then asking questions in regard to what we do in worship, or in order to worship, will also include the question of why we are doing it. If we are worshiping ignorantly, not knowing why we do what we do, then the actual quality and authenticity of that worship is in question. Stoessel also notes that this idea of being "*renewed in the spirit of your mind*" is "part of a thorough reorientation of life in accordance with the truth learned in Christ. However, the Christian [mind] is primarily determined by the acknowledgment of the Lordship of Christ crucified, from which comes acceptance of the cross as a way of life."[11] This gives a unique and far-reaching meaning to the words of Jesus: "*If anyone wishes to come after me, let him deny himself, and take up his cross, and follow Me*" (Matthew 16:24). These words of Jesus show the center point of a lifestyle of worship, and the overall commitment to His way of life.

Worship in Life

Returning to Romans 12, another key to understanding the significance of this passage in reference to worship is found in the next few verses. Paul does not leave us in the dark as to how we are to present our bodies as a "*spiritual service of worship.*" In fact, he gets very specific in detailing exactly the kinds of activities he is talking about. Believe it or not, it is much more extensive than what you generally experience in church on Sunday. Actually, there are people worshiping God right now and they are not singing, praying, or listening to a sermon. Let us find out what Paul means.

Commentators see Romans 12:1-2 as a transition from doctrinal considerations to how this set of beliefs works in daily life (or "practical" application). This becomes glaringly apparent as quickly as verse three where Paul encourages "*sound judgment*" in our thought life about ourselves in comparison with others. *"God,"* he says, *"has allotted to each a measure of faith."* And with that statement he sets the stage for us to comprehend the variety, unity, and complexity of worship within the Body of Christ (i.e., remember that the "body of Christ" is one of Paul's primary pictures for the church—the community of believers. (See also 1 Corinthians 12; Colossians 1:18)

Paul then explains some of the basics of the proper functioning of the Body of Christ. There are many members (individual Christians, vs. 4) and yet only one body (the church, vs. 5). Each individual has been given a measure of faith (vs. 3) to serve others (vss. 5 and 6). The grace and faith given, however, is not in equal measure for some have more, some less, but just as much as is necessary for the individual (see vs. 6), and each member has a different function, or a different job to do (vs. 4). With these differing and numerous functions, or gifts, we serve one another, and the gifts Paul lists are set in the context of use within the community of believers, for he uses the phrase *"one another"* three times before the end of the chapter.

This is the full circle of worship in Romans 12. We are to present our bodies for service to the community of believers based upon our renewed and transformed minds. In so doing, we worship individually by exercising our spiritual gifts, and we worship corporately as the community works together to serve each other and the people around them. When a local representation of the Body of Christ functions in this way it is a marvelous thing—and it is extremely effective. Paul says, in Ephesians 4:16, that *"the proper working of each individual part* (i.e., the Christian serving in his or her giftedness), *causes the growth of the body* (i.e., the Church) *for the building up of itself in love."* Of course it would be this way: God thought of it after all!

An example of this interplay of individual worship based upon spiritual gifts and service to the Body of Christ would be my act of writing this book. Right now, as I work on this paragraph, I am sitting in a library in a corner by myself. I am singing no "Praise and Worship" songs, no hymns, and as far as I can tell there is no sermon being preached anywhere nearby. And, no, I am not witnessing to the person in the cubicle beside me either (actually, there is no one in that cubicle). I am here writing this book. So, given the limited ideas of worship that many people have, they would not describe me as being involved in "worship."

In the more encompassing approach that I have described above, however, I am quite involved in worship. In fact, I consider the activity I am involved in at this moment to be one of my more significant acts of personal/individual worship. Why? How can I say that? Because in my worldview of worship I am applying the gifts God has given to serve the Body of Christ. He has allotted to me some creativity, an enjoyment of studying and teaching, and an ability to write down my thoughts effectively. So, as I use those gifts (His mercies and grace to me, in a measure appropriate for the task), I develop these ideas and write this book in order to offer it to encourage, teach, and foster dialogue in the church, the Body of Christ.

For me, this is where the "rubber meets the road" in worship. This is worship beyond Sunday and infiltrating into my daily life. It is the presentation of my body as a *"spiritual service of worship."* In its truest form, this is the widest ranging idea that we can consider as "worship"—*a **lifestyle in which God is honored and we serve Him daily, moment by moment**.*

There may be some of you who are authors, or could be, so you may actually join me in this form of worship. However, even then our work will be unique, as God has gifted us with mercy and grace appropriate for the task, and we both can serve the Body of Christ in this way. Diversity in unity is a key factor in the operation of the church.

Others may have no inclination to write, or research, or do anything of the sort. What is it that God has given you to do? I have a friend who loves to see the church building clean. It is like his mission in life. He is passionate about vacuuming and loves clean windows. There may be others who can vacuum, and some who can clean windows—even I can do that! But his internal joy at doing it, and his gifting from God, works to produce actions that go beyond average. This is worship at its best as he serves God by serving the Body of Christ with his gifts. To use a popular phrase, my friend in his cleaning has a "heart of worship."

"As exhilarating, burden-lifting, and life-transforming as worship in our services can be," T.D. Jakes writes, "this is only a part of the meaning of worship for the believer. Worship comprises the very essence and foundation of our life in Christ. Worship is the complete consecration of our lives to God. It is the attitude we walk in, speak from, and meditate in at all times. Our life is completely and totally His."[12]

Holistic Worship

It is only as the individual holistically presents body and mind to God in worship that the community can then operate properly, and worship as a group (i.e., corporate worship). This connection between the proper functioning of each part of the Body of Christ through spiritual giftedness and the worship of the community is too often missed, yet appears quite clearly in Romans 12. The truest form of worship is when each Christian, and thus each community, is doing and acting as God created it to do and act (further comments on that concept found in the discussion of Psalm 19 in Chapter 4).

Ronald Allen and Gordon Borror state it this way:

All of life, for the believer, is to be an act of worship. Throughout Scripture this is emphasized. The Jewish nation again and again was commanded to remain pure before God in worship and loyalty. Work was to be an act of worship; marriage, interpersonal relationships, community dealings, and, of course, the entire religious-sacrificial system were to be purely observed to God's glory.[13]

In Romans 15, Paul underscores this idea and points to service (vs. 2), unity (vs. 6), and variety (vs. 7) as core elements of the success of the community to *"glorify the God and Father of our Lord Jesus Christ."*

It is within this broad framework in Romans 12 that we can then form a foundation which will hold true to both the core of what worship means for the community, and the variety that its members can bring to the public setting (as exemplified in the diversity of spiritual giftedness). Christianity is unique in this ability to grasp firmly the core of its belief system, yet provide a wide enough framework for cultural and stylistic differences to flourish. This idea may seem threatening to some, yet it is the very essence that has allowed the Church to flex with all that it has experienced throughout the centuries.

Worship Through Romans

Although I have identified Romans 12:1-2 as a central passage for building a solid foundation (or a framework) for all that worship is to be in our lives, we can also look to the entire book of Romans and see a clear picture for a broad-based perspective on worship. The following points appear to build toward Romans 12 and show the results of this life of worship later in the book of Romans.

Let me first say that worship as it appears in Romans may have been a deliberate sub-theme Paul placed within the book, or it may just be the result of Paul's overall perspective on the Christian life as a lifestyle of worship. He shows how it intertwines with the realities of our daily lives based on the wider perspective he has as an expert and interpreter of the Old Testament. His special understanding of Israel's stunted relationship with God, as well as God's gracious gift of salvation to the Gentiles, is evident throughout the entire book of Romans.

Essentially there is a four-fold consideration of worship within Romans that can be delineated in the following way:

The Focus of Worship (Romans 1:18-32)
The Faith of Worship (Romans 4:19-5:11)
The Form of Worship (Romans 12:1-8)
The Fellowship of Worship (Romans 15:1-7)

These four principles paint an extensive portrait of what worship is to be, and not be, in the realm of human experience.

25

The Focus of Worship

For the wrath of God is revealed from heaven against all ungodliness and unrighteousness of men, who suppress the truth in unrighteousness, because that which is known about God is evident within them; for God made it evident to them. For since the creation of the world His invisible attributes, His eternal power and divine nature, have been clearly seen, being understood through what has been made, so that they are without excuse.

For even though they knew God, they did not honor (glorify) Him as God, or give thanks; but they became futile in their speculations, and their foolish heart was darkened. Professing to be wise, they became fools, and exchanged the glory of the incorruptible God for an image in the form of corruptible man and of birds and four-footed animals and crawling creatures. (Romans 1:18-23)

Romans 1:18-23 is a well-known description of man's innate understanding that there is something, or Someone, beyond himself. Deep within the heart of man is a yearning and searching for meaning. This search can only be accomplished when man's spirit is united with the Creator. As St. Augustine famously wrote, "You stir man to take pleasure in praising you, because you have made us for yourself, and our heart is restless until it rests in you."[14]

Only when the soul rests in God is the yearning satisfied, yet our search is hindered by sin. The rest that Adam enjoyed with God in the garden was shattered through his pride and disobedience. The resulting separation from God—the damaged relationship between God and mankind—extends to each of us today, and yet it is the continued search for this most significant of relationships that consumes our innermost being.

Paul acknowledges this scenario as he begins his discussion in Romans. We can perceive that his mind is centered on the ideas of worship and glorifying God, for his vocabulary is full of such references. He speaks of *"honoring"* or *"glorifying"* God (1:21) and the *"glory of the incorruptible God"* (1:23). He notes how humanity *"worshiped"* and *"served,"* which denotes the concepts of commitment and focus (1:25).

Rather than being a presentation of properly focused worship, Paul is describing the **wrong focus** in these first few verses of Romans. Humanity's sin has so blinded each person that there is no end to the lusts and desires that promote self. Rather than listening to the voice of God found both within themselves (1:19) and without (1:20), they pursue their own lusts and pleasures and their hearts are perpetually darkened (1:21).

This darkened heart leads man continually away from God. Paul even directly refers to this in 3:11-12, *"There is none who seeks for God; All have turned aside..."* Man has become wise in his own eyes and exchanged the true worship and service of the incorruptible God for *"an image in the form of corruptible man and of birds and four-footed animals and crawling creatures"* (1:23). Mankind is addicted to idolatry and seeks to fill the inner yearning with everything other than God Himself.

If there seems to be a stark contrast between the ways of sinful man and the ways of God in these verses, it is because there *is* a stark contrast. God's ways and wisdom are wholly different than sinful humanity's, and the ways of sinful man are always to turn away from God in pursuit of his own desires. Look at the opposites that Paul uses even in these few short verses: suppressed truth (v. 18) and revealed truth (v. 19); clear knowledge about God (v. 20) and futile speculations (v. 21); clear sight (v. 20) and darkened (v. 21); wisdom and foolishness (v. 22); the reality of God and the image of creatures (v. 23); and the incorruptible and the corruptible (v. 23).

Later in the book, Paul contrasts the freedom and redemption in Christ, as signified by the gospel, and the power of sin and death in the law. This is the contrast of law and gospel. For some theologians this is especially significant, and Martin Luther allows it to infiltrate his entire theological perspective for good reason: he finds it in Paul's epistles and Romans in particular. "According to Luther, the preservation of pure doctrine absolutely depends on the accurate theological statement of the nature and meaning of both law and gospel; they must be carefully distinguished and their true relationship to each other must be rightly understood."[15]

Paul continues in Romans chapter one:

> *Therefore God gave them over in the lusts of their hearts to impurity, that their bodies might be dishonored among them. For they exchanged the truth of God for a lie, and worshiped and served the creature rather than the Creator, who is blessed forever. Amen.*
>
> *For this reason God gave them over to degrading passions; for their women exchanged the natural function for that which is unnatural, and in the same way also the men abandoned the natural function of the woman and burned in their desire toward one another, men with men committing indecent acts and receiving in their own persons the due penalty of their error.*
>
> *And just as they did not see fit to acknowledge God any longer, God gave them over to a depraved mind, to do those things which are not proper, being filled*

with all unrighteousness, wickedness, greed, evil; full of envy, murder, strife, deceit, malice; they are gossips, slanderers, haters of God, insolent, arrogant, boastful, inventors of evil, disobedient to parents, without understanding, untrustworthy, unloving, unmerciful; and, although they know the ordinance of God, that those who practice such things are worthy of death, they not only do the same, but also give hearty approval to those who practice them. (Romans 1:24-32)

The results of idolatry and misplaced worship were, and continue to be, devastating for humanity and his broken relationship with the Creator God. The effects of this broken relationship are tragic and ongoing. Paul uses the phrase *"God gave them over"* three times to describe the results of man's rejection of God's love and activity among them.

First, *"God gave them over in the lusts of their hearts to impurity, that their bodies might be dishonored among them"* (1:24). The deterioration of the body—sickness, disease, and brokenness—is directly the result of sin. Ultimately the body dies, yet it was never meant to. Only because of sin (can we call it misplaced worship?) and its results does this wasting away occur. Worship directed toward self and self-satisfaction is ultimately unsatisfying.

Second, *"God gave them over to degrading passions"* (1:26). This in turn led to promiscuity and homosexuality, and all of the associated problems of this kind of evil lifestyle. The word *"degrading"* should be a clue that promiscuity and homosexuality are steps away from God and his purposes for human relationships. In fact, Paul describes the ultimate results of these lifestyles as *"the due penalty of their error"* (1:27). Again, worship is misplaced and focused toward those who cannot fulfill the yearning.

Thirdly, *"God gave them over to a depraved mind"* (1:28). Note that the first two examples refer to external actions. Now Paul comes full circle and commits the whole man to sinfulness. Remember our discussion of Romans 12 and the importance of the internal and external, as well as the interdependence of the two. Here, Paul describes God as allowing man the fullness—not just of depraved activity—but also of a depraved mind. The cycle of sinfulness and denial of God is complete both internally (mind) and externally (actions). This cycle will continue in human experience without divine intervention to bring health and healing. Paul ultimately shows the divine intervention as personified in Christ.

All of this sinful denial of God and misplaced worship takes place in spite of humanity's knowledge of God the Creator. Paul clearly notes that mankind had every opportunity to acknowledge God as God. He states, *"that which is known about God is evident within them; for God made it evident to them"* (1:19) and that the invisible nature of God was *"clearly seen, being understood through what has been made"* (1:20; see also Psalm 19). He also notes that humanity *"knew God"* (1:21), had access to His truth (1:25), and knew the *"ordinance of God"* (1:32).

In spite of all the evidence, mankind rejected Him and His persistent offers of mercy. There is every indication, as well, that humanity has made this decision willfully and with sufficient knowledge of Who God was and what He was doing. ***There is no other conclusion than to say that humanity, in the person of Adam and ever since, chooses to worship and serve everything and anything other than God.*** The misplaced worship of Adam, as he esteemed his own thoughts and desires higher than God's (otherwise known as *pride*), truly flows in the blood of every one of his children, and though we yearn and search for the fulfillment only God can provide, we willfully wander the other way.

The Faith of Worship—Abraham

In hope against hope [Abraham] believed, in order that he might become a father of many nations, according to that which had been spoken, "So shall your descendants be." And without becoming weak in faith he contemplated his own body, now as good as dead since he was about a hundred years old, and the deadness of Sarah's womb; yet, with respect to the promise of God, he did not waver in unbelief, but grew strong, in faith giving glory to God, and being fully assured that what He had promised, He was able also to perform.

Therefore, also it was reckoned to him as righteousness. (Romans 4:18-22)

Although it is evident that man misplaces, or misdirects, his service and worship when left on his own, there has always been a divine solution to this problem, and that solution remains today. Paul addresses this in a theme that might be considered the main emphasis of Romans—**faith**.

Faith is central in the whole Biblical narrative, commencing right away in Genesis, and Paul uses his knowledge of Scripture to pursue this theme. That we would find a connection here between Paul's discussion of Abraham's faith and the concept of worship is demonstrated in the vocabulary Paul utilizes.

Romans 4 explains the way of faith as exemplified in Abraham. Although he could be considered a man of good works, Abraham's activities and "goodness" were not able to earn God's favor. *"For if Abraham was justified by works, he has something to boast about; but not before God"* (4:2).

This coincides with what we saw in Romans 1. Man's ability to worship and serve God properly was damaged by the Fall, and this is true of Abraham as well.

However, Abraham is held up as one who responded to the evidence of God's mercy around him and believed what he heard and saw. It was this belief—this faith—that allocated God's saving mercy into his life. This is what Paul designates as righteousness (4:3-5). In simpler terms, righteousness is the status of a rightly restored relationship with God. Paul contrasts Abraham's faith in God's word and promises with the lack of faith described in Romans 1. Evidence of God's word and activity were known in both cases, but only acted on by Abraham.

Paul notes that Abraham's faith gave *"glory to God"* (4:20), thus establishing a connection with worship terminology. Abraham's unwavering faith in God's promises is the example of a proper response and appropriately focused worship.

Abraham was around 100 years old when God promised to give him a son, and Sarah's womb was "dead" according to Paul's account (4:19). In truth, all of the odds were against Abraham. He was old, his wife was old, the likelihood of either one of them parenting a child was slim to none, and literally impossible for the two of them to have a child together.

Yet Abraham responded in faith. He did not "listen" to his body or his observations of the deadness of Sarah's womb, but he listened to God's words and believed them. Paul says he did not *"become weak in faith"* (4:19) or *"waver in unbelief"* (4:20), but rather *"grew strong, in faith giving glory to God"* (4:20). Abraham knew, at the deepest part of his being he knew and believed, that what God promised He would be able to perform (4:21). It was this faith, this belief that became the cornerstone of Abraham's righteousness. It is a righteousness based not on his own actions, but upon the Word and promises of God.

That his active faith is true worship can be summarized by Luther's words in commenting on the First Commandment, "If your faith and confidence are right, then likewise your God is the true God. On the other hand, if your confidence is false, if it is wrong, then you have not the true God. For the two, faith and God, have inevitable connection. Now, I say, whatever your heart clings to and confides in, that is really your God."[16] This describes Abraham's faith and response to God's promises.

The Faith of Worship—Us

For while we were still helpless, at the right time Christ died for the ungodly. For one will hardly die for a righteous man; though perhaps for the good man someone would dare even to die. But God demonstrates His own love toward us, in that while we were yet sinners, Christ died for us.

Much more then, having now been justified by His blood, we shall be saved from the wrath of God through Him. For if while we were enemies, we were reconciled to God through the death of His Son, much more, having been reconciled we shall be saved by His life. And not only this, but we exult in God through our Lord Jesus Christ, through whom we have now received the reconciliation. (Romans 5:6-11)

This divine provision of faith, as exemplified by Abraham, comes to us as well through Christ, and Paul proceeds in Romans 5 to draw the parallels between our faith and Abraham's. Again, Paul uses worship related terms. He writes, "*we exult,*" in regards to God Himself and His glory (see 5:2 and 11). This exultation only comes our way by faith and through the work of Christ.

Just like Abraham, all of the odds were against us. Paul describes us as "*still helpless*" and "*ungodly*" (5:6) and "*sinners*" (5:8) when God demonstrated His love through Christ. Not only that, we were actually His enemies when He reconciled us to Himself through the death of His Son (5:10). Even now, as we look at ourselves before God's call in our lives, we must admit the impossible position we were in to draw near to God in any way. In Ephesians, Paul describes us as having "*no hope and without God in the world*" (Ephesians 2:12). This would appear to be a position of complete despair.

Yet, just as Abraham responded in faith and believed God's word and promises, Paul recognizes that we also can respond to God's word and promises by faith. In spite of how things appeared, and our inability on our own to have a relationship with God, He calls us to faith in Christ and to be reconciled with Him (Romans 5:8-11). God's grand "Yes" of Christ and the Gospel trumps the "No" found in the power of sin and the Law, as reflected in Paul's comment in 2 Corinthians 1:20, "*For as many as may be the promises of God, in Him they are yes; wherefore also by Him is our Amen to the glory of God through us.*"[17]

The divine provision and gift of faith helps the believer to grow strong and persevere (5:3-4). This, again, is a direct parallel with Abraham's ability to not waver in his faith in spite of his supposed reality. The progress of our daily salvation (our sanctification) in the Christian life is seen in the development of godly character. Tribulations lead to perseverance, which lead to proven character and hope. God is intimately involved in our growth and progress of faith from beginning to end.

This is also evident in the Trinitarian perspective displayed in Romans 5. We have already noted **God's** work of reconciliation through the work of **Christ** on the cross. Often we overlook the truth in Romans 5:5 which brings the reality of God's love into our daily life, "*because the love of God has been poured out within our hearts through the* **Holy Spirit** *who was given to us.*" This is our security, our absolute confidence in God's word and promises for what we need in our lives. Ephesians 1:13-14 describes the Spirit as the "*down payment*" for the promises of God. Just like Abraham, God will deliver to us the promises He made.

And so, "*we exult...we exult...we exult...*" says Paul (5:2, 3, 11). As our response to God reflects the response of Abraham, we are made righteous beside him. This righteousness is a gift of mercy from the love of God, not because of anything that we have done, but as Paul goes on to say, "*...even so through the obedience of the One the many were made righteous*" (5:19). This is the faith of worship, and our exultation is thanksgiving for what He has given us in Christ!

The Form of Worship

Although we have already spent a considerable amount of time in Romans 12, let me give a quick synopsis of thoughts here to connect it with this larger picture of the book of Romans. These points are similar to those I have already made, though maybe set forth a little differently.

First, we note that the form, or pattern, of worship as we find it in Romans 12 is physical and active. This is what it means to present our bodies (12:1). Appropriately, it comes in Romans **after** the discussion of the **faith** of worship, for the actions of worship must only be a thankful response to a work already completed in us, rather than a way to earn the favor of God. Faith first, then action—just like Abraham!!

Second, we balance the physical and active with the internal. Let me phrase it by saying that the appropriate form of worship comes out of, or is the result of, the right **attitude** about worship. Remember the importance of the *"renewed mind"* and that our activity is always the result of our internal decisions (12:2).

Third, the form of worship is empowered by God. It is God that has gifted His people to serve Him and others. This is why His love has been *"poured out within our hearts through the Holy Spirit"* (Romans 5:5). Our ability to serve God and others is empowered by His indwelling Spirit. Paul's writings are filled with references to the work of the Spirit in our lives, and this is evidenced in Romans 12 as he has *"allotted to each a measure of faith"* (12:3). He has given us what we need for what He is asking us to do.

Fourth, and ultimately, the best form of worship is cooperative. As God has gifted each person, we are then responsible to serve others with those gifts (12:4-8). None of us have all the gifts. We need each other to be complete and serve in the fullness of the Body of Christ. This diversity and unity is vital to the proper working of the church.

The Fellowship of Worship

Now we who are strong ought to bear the weaknesses of those without strength and not just please ourselves. Let each of us please his neighbor for his good, to his edification. For even Christ did not please Himself; but as it is written, "The reproaches of those who reproached You fell upon Me."

For whatever was written in earlier times was written for our instruction, that through perseverance and the encouragement of the Scriptures we might have hope.

Now may the God who gives perseverance and encouragement grant you to be of the same mind with one another according to Christ Jesus; that with one

accord you may with one voice glorify the God and Father of our Lord Jesus Christ.
Wherefore, accept one another, just as Christ also accepted us to the glory of God. (Romans 15:1-7)

We now come to the *finale*, so to speak, of the picture of worship that Paul is painting throughout the book of Romans. We find here the goal to which this path has been leading. Let us remember our steps quickly in shortened form. First, we saw the *focus* of worship to be God and God alone, and the corruption that is a result by misplacing that worship onto idols of any kind—whether man, beast or non-living entity (Romans 1). Then Abraham was presented as an example of true worship. His worship was one of responsive obedience and an unwavering belief that God could and would do what He promised. We referred to this as the *faith* of worship (Romans 4 & 5).

After this, the path led once again to Romans 12 and the reality of worship being both internal and external. This is the *form* of worship that engulfs the whole person and the whole of daily life. And now we come to the *fellowship* of worship, which ultimately signifies the wholeness, not only of each person, but also of the Church, which is Christ's body.

We can examine this goal for living the Christian life in the worship of God in Paul's words in Ephesians 4:13. Paul indicates that the point of the lifestyle of worship within the Church is to *"attain to the unity of the Son of God, to a mature man, to the measure of the stature which belongs to the fullness of Christ."* Although we find this concise phrase describing the results of a healthy Church life in Ephesians, we also find this end goal for our worship described in Romans 15:1-7.

As before, we discover Paul using worship terminology to discuss the fellowship of Christians loving and serving one another. He is expecting the combined Christian effort of living godly lives to issue forth in a unity of purpose and voice. *"That with one accord you may with one voice glorify the God and Father of our Lord Jesus Christ"* (15:6). Obviously, from the perspective of the larger context, our unified "voice" is not necessarily vocal but a reflection of our daily lives of obedience and service (i.e., faith). As Vigen Guroian observes, "The word liturgy [i.e., the service of the people] derives from the Greek *leitourgia*. The Greek connotes an action through which persons come together to become something corporately which they were not as separate individuals. It means a gathering whose unifying purpose is to serve (minister to) the world on behalf of God."18

In this pattern of the worship life, we are to be others focused. Paul refers to our *"neighbor"* (15:2) and his or her needs as that which determines our activity. He even points to Christ as an example of this outward focus (15:3). It is clear here, and in other places, that **the life of worship is one of actively serving God by serving others**. James indicates this in his epistle when he says, *"Show me your faith **without** the works, and I will show you my faith **by** my works"* (James 2:18). I am not saying that a verbal and community time of "worship" (i.e., a worship service) is unimportant, but that in the broad sense of the idea of worship in Scripture it is only a part.

Paul also has the expectation that we will be committed to the body of Christ, forgiving and loving one another as God forgave and loved us (15:7). This matter of loving, forgiving, and persevering with and for one another draws the body together. Paul says it leads to the *"same mind"* (15:5) with *"one accord"* and *"one voice"* (15:6). This is unity. Unity in diversity, as mentioned before, is a hallmark of the Body of Christ. We differ in our giftedness and abilities, yet serve toward the same purpose—bringing glory (worship) to God.

38

Of course, Paul reiterates the "renewal of the mind" (12:2) idea in 15:4 when he states, *"For whatever was written in earlier times was written for our instruction, that through perseverance and the encouragement of the Scriptures we might have hope."* It is no accident that Paul reuses phrases and terms we have already discussed in previous sections. His thought is interconnected throughout Romans, and his desire is that the Body of Christ becomes a community of loving individuals unified in their service to God, and also that God would be glorified in what we do.

And so we see that worship is an integral theme within the book of Romans. It would be unique if it only appeared here, but we will see that these concepts cross through many of Paul's writings as well as the other writers of the New Testament—and they are founded upon principles laid down in the Old Testament. This is why it is important to **think** properly about worship, that we may then experience a life of worship, which encompasses the whole of our daily lives.

Worship in the Old Testament

The implications of Romans 12 as discussed in chapter one, as well as the overall picture of worship as presented in chapter two, are broad-based and life encompassing. The reader might think I have gone too far in assigning so much meaning to such a small portion of Scripture without recognizing, for example, the large amount of teaching in the Old Testament about worship. I would chance a guess that a large majority of the writings about worship begins with a discussion of the Old Testament patterns, and so for me to open my study in Romans may be seen as unusual. Let me put your mind at ease.

As mentioned previously, every facet of life in Israel was to be considered part of the overall worship life of the nation. Granted, there were specific rules and regulations to follow in regards to the actual "public" worship of the nation as entrusted to the priestly tribe of the Levites. Yet, there is an underlying set of principles—a solid foundation or framework—for worship that helps all of those specifics make sense. That underlying set of principles (i.e., worldview) is the point of this chapter, and as you will see, parallels the model set forth from Romans 12.

First, let me quote Deuteronomy 10:12-21. If it is your habit to skip long quotes such as this one, please consider reading this one carefully. The concepts and ideas Moses presents in this passage are profound and vital to understanding what was expected from Israel living as God's people on a day-to-day basis, and by extension in related ideas in the New Testament, what is expected of members of the Body of Christ as well.

The scene for these words of Moses is that of Israel standing ready to enter the Promised Land. Israel had been rescued by God from captivity in Egypt, wandered in the desert for forty years due to their obstinate heart and disobedient ways, and was now poised to claim this *"land flowing with milk and honey."* Moses takes time in Deuteronomy to remind the people of their journey, to recall the faithfulness of God toward Israel, and to re-read the Law given to them by God. As Moses does so, he encourages and challenges them by saying:

> *And now, Israel, what does the Lord your God require from you, but to fear the Lord your God, to walk in all His ways and love Him, and serve the Lord your God with all your heart and with all your soul, and to keep the Lord's commandments and His statutes which I am commanding you today for your good?*
>
> *Behold, to the Lord your God belong heaven and the highest heavens, the earth and all that is in it. Yet on your fathers did the Lord set His affections to love them, and He chose their descendants after them, even you above all peoples, as it is this day.*
>
> *Circumcise then your heart, and stiffen your neck no more. For the Lord your God is the God of gods and the Lord of lords, the great, the mighty, and the awesome God who does not show partiality, nor take a bribe. He executes justice for the orphan and the widow, and shows His love for the alien by giving him food and clothing.*
>
> *So show your love for the alien, for you were aliens in the land of Egypt. You shall fear the Lord your God; you shall serve Him and cling to Him, and you shall swear by His name. He is your praise and He is your God, who has done these great and awesome*

things for you which your eyes have seen.
(Deuteronomy 10:12-21)

Before focusing on specifics, note the overriding sense of what Moses is saying. It is God who chose Israel. It is God who rescued them. It is God who provided for them and cares for them. ***This is, in truth, the most basic and fundamental principle of worship: God has acted to establish a relationship with man in love, care, and redemption, and man's response to Him is to be one of fear, love, and obedience.*** God is the initiator; man is the responder. Worship is best when it is the thankful response of obedience to God for His grace and mercy in our lives. But what does this response look like? In what way was Israel to respond, and thereby worship the Lord in life?

Fear, Love and Trust

This passage in Deuteronomy reminds me of Martin Luther's admonitions in his Catechisms to *fear*, *love* and *trust* God in all of life. The first of the Ten Commandments reads, *"I am the Lord your God, who brought you out of the land of Egypt, out of the house of slavery. You shall have no other gods before Me"* (Exodus 20:2-3). Luther was a professor of Old Testament studies, and based upon his reading of the first commandment, he saw that fear, love, and trust were based upon the character of the object being feared, loved, and trusted.[19] To have *"no other gods"* besides the one God is a response of faith to the promise of God to be a Father to His children. Once this relationship is properly established, and believed in faith, the other commandments and the life of worship Moses is calling for flows from the love of Christ and love for our neighbors, rather than from the burden of laws and requirements.

The word *fear* refers to the recognition and awe of God in His greatness, but also fear in the realization that God is so great and His children so unworthy. It is not a condemning fear, but an understanding that we are utterly incapable of earning His favor and only stand before Him out of His grace and the work and righteousness of Christ.

Love for God is responsiveness to His love for His children. God's provision of every need as our Father and the Preserver of all things comes to His children out of His grace, based upon no merit of their own. All that we have and call our own are gifts of our Father: self, family, friends, property, good government, employment, peace, health, good weather, etc. Everything within and without are from God and our response should be one of thankfulness.

We are to *trust* in God as a child trusts a father. We are to find refuge and safety in Him and His provision. This faith, or trust, should have as its object the One that determines the core of our identity—it determines who we are. If this faith is misplaced, our identity is misplaced, but when centered upon God and His grace, then we have the gift of the right object of faith, the Lord Jesus Christ.

At a very basic and underlying level this *fear, love*, and *trust* of God gives us perspective. In fact, it gives us a balanced perspective in every area of life. When we truly understand who God is, how He cares for His people, and how He loves and provides for us we also begin to understand who we are as His children. We are entirely dependent upon Him for all good things and owe Him our gratitude, our service, and our livelihood. In this balanced perspective, the response of worship encompasses ***our entire lifestyle*** so that work, play, love for family and friends, corporate worship services, and everything else ***become an interwoven tapestry of worship and declaration of God's glory***.

Responding in Daily Worship

Note in Deuteronomy 10:12 that Moses asks the question: *"What does the Lord your God require of you?"* He responds with parallel thoughts as described above. Israel's response was to be based upon a balanced perspective of who God was and what He had done for them as a nation, as well as understanding who they were in relationship to Him, and their need of God as Provider and Sustainer. They were to fear God, love God, serve God, and trust His continuing provision and care. It was to be a total and complete commitment of *"all your heart and all your soul."*

This is a description of the everyday life for the Israelite. Moses is depicting a lifestyle of worship: defined as fearing God, walking in His ways, loving Him, serving Him and keeping His commandments and statutes. Modern discussions often break down in failing to recognize the complete scope (beyond the public worship event) that this passage (among others) establishes as the norm for everyday life. Only when we regain this broader perspective will we truly understand what the life of worship involves.

Honoring God in Public Worship

This is not to say that there is no need to focus some energy, study, and planning for the corporate worship event. There are obvious indications that this is the case in both the Old and New Testaments. One important example in the Old Testament is the tragic story of Eli's sons, the priests Hophni and Phinehas (1 Samuel 1:1-4:11). The writer of 1 Samuel tells us that they *"were worthless men; they did not know the Lord and the custom of the priests with the people...for the men despised the offering of the Lord"* (1 Samuel 2:12-13; 17). For their unbelieving hearts and disobedience in the practice of worship, and for taking advantage of God's people, they eventually lost their lives as God judged them.

The story of Hophni and Phinehas is deeper than simply their personal judgment and death. Scripture underscores the heart of the matter when a *"man of God"* confronts Eli the priest as the father of these disobedient sons. God removes His blessing from Eli and his entire household because Eli honored his sons more than he honored God (1 Samuel 2:29). We could say he misplaced his worship, reminding us of our discussion concerning Romans 1. Yes, Eli had confronted his sons about their unbelief and sin (1 Samuel 2:22-25), but instead of being a spiritual leader of Israel and of his family by removing them from priestly office, he allowed them to continue in their sin, and to lead others into sin. This is a grave example of "proclaimed" internal beliefs and external actions being inconsistent, and an all-too-common reality in the life of Israel as a whole. In fact, the real internal beliefs were absolutely consistent with the external results, neither of which were honoring to God. Eli honored his sons more than God.

So, although it appears Hophni and Phinehas were judged for their improper worship practices (i.e. public worship event), at a deeper level God's judgment was based upon the internal belief system that moved their actions into reality. It is the writer of 1 Samuel that said, *"Man looks at the outward appearance, but the Lord looks at the heart"* (1 Samuel 17:7). God's vision is deeper than simply examining what we do, He sees through to what we are and what we believe, so our internal belief system (i.e., our theology) is of vital concern.

A New Testament Example

In the New Testament, Ananias and Sapphira give us a comparable example. Acts 5:1-5 reads:

> *But a certain man named Ananias, with his wife Sapphira, sold a piece of property, and kept back some of the price for himself, with his wife's full knowledge, and bringing a portion of it, he laid it at the apostles' feet.*
>
> *But Peter said, "Ananias, why has Satan filled your heart to lie to the Holy Spirit, and to keep back some of the price of the land? While it remained unsold, did it not remain your own? And after it was sold, was it not under your control? Why is it that you have conceived this deed in your heart? You have not lied to men, but to God."*
>
> *And as he heard these words, Ananias fell down and breathed his last; and great fear came upon all who heard of it.*

Ironically, Sapphira entered only a little while later, not realizing her husband had been judged, and found the same fate. It is evident within the context of this narrative that Ananias and his wife were seeking to look good in the eyes of those around them. But God saw their hearts and judged them according to the intent of their hearts. Their public expression of "worship" was a lie, although it probably appeared really generous to the crowd. God did not care how it looked, but was concerned with what was going on in their inner beings.

Internal and External

The primary focus in many modern discussions about worship is the public, corporate worship event/service, yet Scripture clearly teaches that *the corporate event is only part of the whole picture of worship as set forth in the Bible.* The result of this unbalanced focus has led to some oversight in reference to a solid, balanced view of worship that encompasses a person's entire lifestyle. To use Schaeffer's internal-external terminology: the **external** expression and activity of worship, when focused too narrowly on the corporate event, is not consistent with a proper **internal** understanding of an all-encompassing and broader expectation of worship as a lifestyle, as it is found in Scripture.

The passage in Deuteronomy 10, quoted earlier, is an excellent example of both internal and external characteristics of worship. What does Moses ask? *"And now, Israel, what does the Lord your God require from you?"* (Deuteronomy 10:12) There is an echo of this question in the Westminster Catechism as well. The question: *"What is the chief end of man?"* The answer: *"To glorify God and enjoy Him forever."* These questions and their answers are related for they invoke an internal response as mentioned earlier in the fear, love, and trust of God. Fear, love, and trust also have external expressions and Moses shows this in his comments.

Moses is sure to develop fully, yet concisely, the character of God. He is first of all the *"Lord"* to Whom belongs the heavens, the earth, and all that they contain (Deuteronomy 10:14). He is full of mercy and love toward Israel in spite of their lowly status as a nation (vs. 15, 22). He is the *"God of gods and the Lord of lords, the great, the mighty, and the awesome God"* (vs. 17). He loves impartially and is not swayed in establishing justice for the widow, orphan, and alien (vs. 17-18). It is this God, Whose character is unquestionable, who has *"done these great and awesome things for you which your eyes have seen"* (vs. 21).

Moses also helps the Israelites maintain a proper perspective on themselves. It was nothing that they, or their ancestors, had done to earn God's favor, but only His love and mercy that brought His affection on them (vs. 15). In fact, they were stubborn and often unrepentant (vs. 16). It was they who were the "*aliens*" in Egypt whom God redeemed from captivity (vs. 19). All things said, God's love and providential care for Israel had nothing to do with them (for their character was questionable) or what they had done, but was entirely dependent upon God's character and choice of them (vs. 21-22).

And as His chosen people they are to emulate His character (internal) and actively love their neighbor (external). They are to be, in their everyday life and livelihood—in their families, occupations, and dealings with all men—representing the activity of God among men, just as God was active in the midst of Israel. The internal elements of love, fear, and total devotion of heart are intertwined with the external characteristics of walking in His ways, serving Him, keeping His commandments and statutes, showing love for the alien (and the widow, orphan, and neighbor), clinging to Him, and living in praise of Him.

Commenting on a similar passage in Deuteronomy 6:4-9, Josh McDowell comments:

> With those words, Moses was not only proclaiming the truth, he was calling for a "lived-out" truth – a way of life. Moses called for God's people to both orthodoxy (right beliefs) *and* orthopraxy (right actions) in a way that tied the two things intrinsically together, making the truth an integrated, relational part of everyday life.[20]

Moses cannot be more emphatic or inclusive in his description of the totally committed life. It is a life of worship. Furthermore, we can see the obvious parallels between this Old Testament passage and the New Testament passage considered from Romans 12. This passage in Deuteronomy indicates Moses' attitude about worship that was also reflected by Paul.

T.D. Jakes summarizes this point well:

To Paul, worship was not something he did occasionally as a ritual or special event; it was something he did continually. Following his example, worship of our God must not be something we do with one aspect of our being, such as our voice; it is something we must do with all that we are. Worship of our God is not accomplished in services from time to time; *worship is our service.* Nor is worship something we do only when we are happy and blessed. We worship God in all situations and circumstances.[21]

The Heavens Declare

Psalm 19 seems to me the next best step in our consideration of a Biblical and broad-based framework for worship. Once we begin to understand the underlying principles of worship found in the book of Romans, as well as Deuteronomy 10, we can build upon those principles by expanding and deepening our study of various aspects.

With those principles established in the previous chapters, Psalm 19 comes to us as broadening a specific concept of worship, and a very important one at that. The first few verses read as follows:

> *The heavens are telling of the glory of God;*
> *And their expanse is declaring the work of His hands.*
> *Day to day pours forth speech,*
> *And night to night reveals knowledge.*
> *There is no speech, nor are their words;*
> *Their voice is not heard.*
> *Their sound has gone out through all the earth,*
> *And their utterances to the end of the world.*
> (Psalm 19:1-4a)

This is quite an interesting passage in relationship to worship. Note that David, the Psalmist in this case, uses the phrase *"telling of the glory of God"* to describe the worship that God's creation gives to Him. I actually like the various translations (NIV, KJV and others) that express it this way: *"The heavens **declare** the glory of God."* The created universe is an active participant in ***declaring*** God's glory. In other words, creation worships its Creator.

David proceeds to adopt a literary device called **personification** in which human characteristics are employed to describe inanimate objects. In this way he writes, "*the heavens are telling,*" the "*expanse is declaring,*" the day "*pours forth speech,*" and the night "*reveals knowledge.*" The nature of this type of figure of speech is that it is understood that these created objects do not actually speak or tell, yet we can still "hear" something from them.

Other Psalmists have utilized similar devices in their references to creation's praise of its Maker. Note the use of these poetic devices in Psalm 96:11-13a:

> *Let the heavens be glad, and let the earth rejoice;*
> *Let the sea roar, and all it contains;*
> *Let the field exult, and all that is in it.*
> *Then all the trees of the forest will sing for joy*
> *Before the Lord, for He is coming...*

And in Psalm 98:7-9a:

> *Let the sea roar, and all it contains,*
> *The world and those who dwell in it.*
> *Let the rivers clap their hands;*
> *Let the mountains sing together for joy*
> *Before the Lord, for He is coming...*

These are rich and beautiful expressions of creation as it speaks and declares God's glory—or we might say—as creation worships!

David Clarifies His Meaning

David immediately follows his own use of this poetic device in Psalm 19 by clarifying what he means. In verse three he states, *"There is no speech, nor are their words; Their voice is not heard."* While the created things he mentions somehow "speak" to us, and we have a message to "hear" from them, they do not actually have a voice, nor do they use words to communicate.

Still, verse four tells us that the way these objects of creation communicate their worship of God is quite effective, for their message flows *"through all the earth"* and *"to the end of the world."* No modern day preacher using simulcast technology and broadcasting on TV, radio, Internet and satellite, and even the pod-cast can claim such a far-reaching proclamation. This description of creation's worship of God explains something that is truly unique!

So, how does it happen? What exactly are the heavens doing to *"declare the glory of God?"* How does the expanse declare *"the work of His hands?"* What form of communication is the creation employing that is so effective and expansive? If David makes it a point to use the technique of personification, then to explain it as such, what is he telling us about worship? What can we learn from creation about worship and how we might also worship?

We could answer these questions by noting that all of creation shows God's glory by evidence of intelligent design. This is true. Recent scholarship in the debate with Darwinian Evolution continues to erode the tenets of evolution and re-establish the truth of a creation designed and implemented by an Intelligent Designer.[22] It seems, however, that this would be too limiting in David's mind and that he wants us to go further than that in our understanding of how creation declares God's glory in Psalm 19.

Let me ask a leading question and take you through to an interesting conclusion: What are the heavens (the created things) *doing* to declare God's glory? In other words, what are they *doing* to worship God and spread His message? David makes it clear that they are not speaking their message with words or voice, so their declaration is based upon something else. They must be showing the glory of God. These created objects are *doing actions that worship him* and are proclaiming His message.

We see in verses 4b-6 that David describes the action of the sun as it rises at *"one end of the heavens"* and follows its circuit *"to the other end of them."* This is a specific example of how the heavenly bodies declare God's glory and spread the message of the Creator, for *"there is nothing hidden from its heat."*

So, when asking the question: What are the heavens (the created things) *doing* to declare God's glory? My answer would simply be that *they are doing what God created them to do*. In other words, God's creation shows His glory (i.e., worships) by being what God created it to be and fulfilling its God-given mission. The sun worships by shining and by faithfully following its daily circuit. The flower worships by growing and being beautiful. The stars worship by shining in the night sky. The fish worship by swimming (and being deep fried!). The trees worship by swaying and providing oxygen. *When the created things declare His glory by being what God created them to be and doing what God created them to do – they are worshiping!*

This explains how God's creation can *"declare"* and *"tell"* and *"speak"* without using words or speech. This also explains how the message of creation, when declaring God's glory, is so widespread and far-reaching. Everyone sees them. No one is hidden from the sun, the moon, and the sky. North to South, East to West, throughout the entire globe the effects of these heavenly bodies speak to humanity—and we hear though there is no voice. This is also what Paul was referring to in Romans 1:20 when he wrote, *"For since the creation of the world His invisible attributes, His eternal power and divine nature, have been clearly seen, being understood through what has been made, so that they are without excuse."*

The Heavens Declare

I like to call this whole idea *The Heavens Declare Principle: Worship at its fundamental state takes place when God's creation honors (or worships) Him by being what it was created to be and doing what it was created to do.* Note the aspects of internal (being) and the external (doing). This is an all-encompassing definition of worship that must serve as the basis for any discussion of the narrower focus of public worship and fits snugly with the underlying principles found in Romans 12 and Deuteronomy 10.

When we consider the larger picture of how God's creation is declaring His glory, we then can see where man has his place in the worship of God. Drawing this principle further, we can see that man, as the bearer of God's image, declares God's glory by also doing what he was created to do. He is to subdue and rule the earth. This would be to fulfill what is called the Cultural Mandate. The fact that sin has infected and distorted this process has diminished its effect, but does not destroy the "mannishness" that still brings God glory. As Schaeffer comments, "A Christian knows that this is because man has been made in the image of God and though man is fallen, separated from God by his true guilt, yet nevertheless he has not become a machine."[23] This is what redemption is all about.

Nancy Pearcey brings this into perspective when she writes,

> The lesson of the Cultural Mandate is that our sense of fulfillment depends on engaging in creative, constructive work. The ideal human existence is not eternal leisure or an endless vacation—or even a monastic retreat into prayer and meditation—but creative effort expended for the glory of God and the benefit of others. Our calling is not just to 'get to heaven' but also to cultivate the earth, not just to 'save souls' but also to serve God through our work. For God Himself is engaged not only in the work of salvation (special grace) but also in the work of preserving and developing His creation (common grace). When we obey the Cultural Mandate, we participate in the work of God Himself, as agents of His common grace.[24]

You can see that Pearcey is adopting terminology similar to that of David's in Psalm 19. Redeemed humanity (i.e., the Christian) declares God's glory, or worships, by obeying and fulfilling the Cultural Mandate. As discussed in Romans 12, worship is the active presentation of our bodies for God's glory and for the service of others based upon right thinking. This does not mean that every Christian, or any Christian, does this perfectly and effectively because our nature is fallen and corrupted by sin along with all of humanity. It is, however, to be the goal and focus of our lives to move in this direction.

Pearcey continues by saying, "This is the rich content that should come to mind when we hear the word *Redemption*. The term does not refer only to a one-time conversion event. It means entering upon a lifelong quest to devote our skills and talents to building things that are beautiful and useful, while fighting the forces of evil and sin that oppress and distort the creation."[25]

Again, this is an all-encompassing worship that draws all of our activity under the Lordship of Jesus Christ. Do you work in the fields or the factory? Does your office consist of a gray-walled cubicle or fancy inlayed hardwoods? Is your work physical or is it primarily office work? Are you a stay-at-home mom, or a single parent juggling kids and work?

Take the time to consider your life as a life of worship. A mother caring for her family is thoroughly involved in worship as she feeds and bathes the baby, launders the fifteenth load of laundry this week, and strives to offer balanced meals on a daily basis. She honors God in faithfully fulfilling her calling to care for her family in these, and a myriad of other ways. She will declare God's glory more by her character than anything she could say to those who observe her. In this she is actively living **The Heavens Declare Principle**. Each of us, in our callings in life, must strive to live the same way, and thus worship God in the midst of our daily lives.

Credit Where Credit is Due

By now you might have noticed that I have been greatly influenced by the writings of Martin Luther, since I have quoted him often. The study of his theology rejuvenated my own theology, as well as deepening my understanding of the Christian life. In re-reading the previous paragraphs, I must give credit where credit is due, for I see his influence wrapped into my own discussion.

I would encourage any believer seeking to live a life that pleases God (a life of worship) to find a copy of Luther's small treatise called *The Freedom of a Christian*, or in some translations, *Christian Liberty*. You will find in this writing an excellent source of wisdom in regards to what it means to live a truly Christian life. A short quote will suffice now, which reads:

> This is the truly Christian life. Here faith is truly active through love (Galatians 5:6), that is, it finds expression in works of the freest service, cheerfully and lovingly done, with which a man willingly serves another without hope of reward; and for himself he is satisfied with the fullness and wealth of his faith.[26]

In the context of his treatise Luther is showing how one might serve God and thank Him in life—by serving the neighbor and the person in need. Luther reiterates the concept that worship is a response of thankfulness to God for what He has given us in Christ, and that that response works itself out in life as we love God by loving our neighbor.

The New Creation

Beyond the concept of fulfilling the Cultural Mandate we must also speak to the concept of the Christian as the New Creation, just as we spoke of the physical creation praising God by being and doing what they were created to be and do. Second Corinthians 5:17 reads, *"Therefore if any man is in Christ, he is a new creature; the old things have passed away; behold, new things have come."* This verse tells us that the redeemed man or woman in Christ is a *"new creature."* By simply drawing a parallel with Psalm 19, we can bring our Christian life into this discussion of *The Heavens Declare Principle*.

After becoming a new creature, and receiving the gift of salvation by God's grace through the work of Christ on the cross, God has implanted within each Christian gifts of the Spirit by which we are to serve Him, His body, and people in general. This was discussed in the chapter on Romans 12. To make the connection clearer still, let me put it this way:

When we become a new creation we take on a new identity as a child of God (internal) and now can use the gifts He gives us to be what we are and do what He created us to do (external), and thus we are worshiping.

So worship should permeate our lives as children of God. The beauty of this idea is that we begin to recognize the value of each person's part in the Body of Christ. The men and women raking leaves in the church lawn, as they use their gifts of service, are worshiping. The men and women who pray unceasingly for the needs of others are worshiping through their gift of intercession. Those that serve in the church office or the kitchen, those who are teachers, helpers, musicians, and others worship God through their giftedness. He is honored (worshiped!) when His body functions as it was intended to function—each of us serving in our area of giftedness. My point is this: just as creation in reality worships by fulfilling its God-designed purpose; thus we, as new creations, worship by fulfilling our God-designed purpose (spiritual giftedeness). Service is worship! (Refer once again to Romans 12:1-2.)

The Pattern for our Mind

In completing our discussion of Psalm 19, we see that David, in a sense, sets the pattern that Paul uses in Romans 12. Verses seven through eleven of the Psalm point to the great benefit of understanding the ways of God—his precepts, commandments, character, etc.

The law of the Lord is perfect, restoring the soul;
The testimony of the Lord is sure,
   making wise the simple.
The precepts of the Lord are right, rejoicing the heart;
The commandment of the Lord is pure,

enlightening the eyes.
The fear of the Lord is clean, enduring forever;
The judgments of the Lord are true;
*   they are righteous all together.*
They are more desirable than gold,
*   yes, than much fine gold;*
Sweeter also than honey
*   and the drippings of the honeycomb.*
Moreover, by them Your servant is warned;
In keeping them there is great reward. (Psalm 19:7-11)

David states that the knowledge of God (internal) and His ways are "*more desirable than gold*" and "*sweeter also than honey.*" Just like Paul, David is speaking of the internal thoughts of a person. Essentially, this is a poetic description of Paul's concept of "*renewing the mind.*"

And, just as Paul does, David completes the principle that the internal thought life determines the shape and activity of the external life. In Psalm 19:11-13, David states that learning God's principles for life (internally) will help keep him on the right track in his daily life (externally). By these principles he is both "warned" and "rewarded." It is his daily life that will improve when guided by the principles for life that God provides in Scripture. He learns the principles (internal) and then lives by those principles (external).

By doing this, David asks God to:

Acquit me of hidden faults.
Also keep back Your servant from presumptuous sins;
Let them not rule over me;
Then I shall be complete,
And I shall be acquitted of great transgressions.
(Psalm 19:12b-13)

God's creation not only tells of His glory, but it also teaches us, as His new creation, that our lives can be full and complete by serving Him. When we fulfill our responsibility as humans, ruling and subduing the earth (the Cultural Mandate), as well as serving God and others by the gifts of the Spirit Who resides within each Christian, we are truly being what God created us to be and doing what God created us to do. We are truly living *The Heavens Declare Principle*.

Jeremy Begbie says it this way:

> The Bible speaks many times of creation praising God; it is our role to extend that worship, to enable creation to glorify its Maker in a way that it could never do if it were left to itself...Our task is not simply to sit back and enjoy creation, but to take what is potential and make it actual: to harvest the sea, plough the ground, harness the elements, and bring forth new forms of order not immediately given "in the beginning." Further, all of this is to be carried out *with others and for the good of others.*[27]

This may be a new line of thinking for you in regards to worship, but I would encourage you to think this through for yourself, as well as for your church. Do you know what your spiritual gift is? If so, are you using it to serve God by serving others? If not, why? God has planned for the church to worship Him by doing what they were created to do. If you're not doing that, then are you really worshiping?

In Spirit and in Truth

Many discussions of worship flow from Jesus' words in John 4:24, *"God is spirit, and those who worship Him must worship in spirit and in truth."* The idea of worshiping *"in spirit and truth"* has hit a nerve in the larger community of the church and among many worship leaders. Although this seems to be a "re-discovery" of an important spiritual truth, the discussion often leads to a limited and subjective practice of worship, as well as worship which is experience oriented rather than balanced and holistic.

In the context of the passage, Jesus is speaking with a Samaritan woman about her own (and her people's) misunderstanding about the worship of God. The Samaritans and Jews were notoriously bickering with one another, since the Jews considered the Samaritan a half-breed: an odd mixture of Jewish descendants and the heathen population of the region of Samaria. The "pure breed" Jews saw them as representing the sin of the Ten Tribes of Israel that broke from the kingdom of David and began to "prostitute" themselves with other nations.[28] Note how the Samaritan woman's comment places worship in the realm of a place: *"Our fathers (the Samaritans) worshiped in this mountain, and you people (the Jews) say that in Jerusalem is the place where men ought to worship"* (John 4:20). Jesus' reply settles the matter:

> *Jesus said to her, 'Woman, believe Me, an hour is coming when neither in this mountain, nor in Jerusalem, shall you worship the Father. You worship that which you do not know; we worship that which we know, for salvation is from the Jews. But*

an hour is coming, and now is, when the true worshipers shall worship the Father in spirit and truth; for such people the Father seeks to be His worshipers. God is spirit, and those who worship Him must worship in spirit and truth. (John 4:21-24)

Nothing New

The contemporary focus on this passage is really nothing new. For example, both John Calvin and Ulrich Zwingli (who, along with Martin Luther, were three of the most significant Reformers in the 16th Century) seized upon this passage to define their views of worship during the Reformation. What is interesting is the stifling results in the area of creativity that this caused for centuries within the Reformed church traditions.

Calvin allowed these verses to confine the use of music in public worship strictly to Psalms (the Psalter) and the few other specific songs found in Scripture. His point was that Christ defined the boundaries of worship in John 4:24 and only what was *"in spirit and truth"* could be properly justified for public use. Because God establishes **truth** through the **Spirit's** work in the writing of Scripture, only Scripture is appropriate for use in worship settings. Music, for Calvin, was to be simple—unison singing of Psalms with no accompaniment.

For Calvin, worship was God's activity among the people in the liturgy and sacraments and, as John Witvliet writes, "this divine action was construed in Trinitarian terms, where Christ is 'the chief conductor of our hymns (i.e., psalms),' the one who 'hallows our lips...to sing the praises of God,' while the Holy Spirit is the prompter who urges the people to sing."[29] This helps us understand why Calvin limited music in the church to that of the Psalms, for he considered the purest form of lyric as coming directly from the hand of God.

Other music and hymns were prohibited because they were "the production of men. God could be worshiped in a worthy manner, according to Calvin's principles, only by hymns which were divinely inspired, namely the psalms of the Old Testament Psalter."[30]

Regardless of the stifling effect upon the corporate worship of the church, Calvin's principles were based upon his theology and what he saw as the underlying Biblical thought for worship. For this he can be truly admired, for his activity of worship followed his internal belief system of worship based upon Scripture. He was consistent.

Zwingli pressed the point even further. He taught that worship *"in spirit and truth"* could only be done through prayer. As a result, the liturgy (i.e., public worship) was to be limited to prayer (which is truly to be *"in spirit"*) and expounding of the Scriptures (where truth is found). Music and any other "ornaments" distorted both the spiritual emphasis and truth of worship. These ornaments would also cause distractions leading away from a focus upon God and His Word, and toward the performers themselves and their talents. This is quite an intriguing theological development from Zwingli, considering he was a musical prodigy who was proficient in the performance of practically any instrument he chose to play!

Zwingli basically omitted music as a whole from the corporate worship of the church. In his view, the use of music for public worship was "scripturally indefensible on three closely related, yet distinguishable, grounds:

- Music in worship is not explicitly commanded by God in either the Old or New Testament;
- Christ instructed men to pray to God individually and in private (John 4:24); and,
- Saint Paul urged men, when together, to worship God and pray to Him in their hearts (Colossians 3:16)."[31]

In this short synopsis, we can perceive that Zwingli was quite consistent in applying his Biblical and theological convictions to his view of worship. From those convictions flowed his practice. This is the right pattern—internal beliefs expressed in external actions. We must follow the same pattern of consistent application as we re-think the Biblical framework for worship in our day.

In regards to how Zwingli read and interpreted John 4:24 he was very clear. He wrote, "But when we wish to pray we should withdraw into our chamber and close the door after us and there, in secret, call upon our heavenly Father."[32] For Zwingli, private, personal prayer was the purest form of being "*in the spirit*." So the truest form of worship, in the very words of Christ, was private, personal prayer. This reduced corporate worship to its very minimal essence of public prayer (the corporate manifestation of "*in the spirit*") along with Scripture reading and preaching (the corporate manifestation of "*in truth*"). Nothing more was permitted, according to this Reformer, for nothing more was commanded by Christ.

The Dialogue Today

Although the current dialogue among worship leaders concerning these verses begins with the phrase "*in spirit and truth*," there does not appear to be a desire to limit the expression of worship like Calvin or Zwingli. In fact, unlike these two Reformers, today's discussion of these verses does not seek a theological foundation, but a methodology. It appears to me that it actually has more to do with the statement found in John 4:23 when Jesus refers to those that worship in spirit and truth as "*such people the Father seeks to be His worshipers*."

Obviously, there is a strong desire in contemporary settings to be someone that "*the Father seeks*." Let us be realistic, what Christian striving to live a truly Christian lifestyle would not like to find himself or herself described as one "*the Father seeks,*" especially in our worship? We could be truly set apart by discovering how to implement this in our worship practices. If we could just do it right, would not the Father be pleased?

The underlying source of this kind of "angst" or "worry" in our worship practice is much deeper and more telling than it appears. A renewal of worship practices that appear to be more spiritually sensitive will not relieve the anxiety that we still might not be worshiping rightly, and therefore missing the mark of being people "*the Father seeks.*" Daily devotions, new forms of congregational worship, the return to traditional or even ancient models of liturgy are at the heart of the discussion, but these things are not the heart of the problem. The heart of the problem, under all the rhetoric, is that Christians do not believe what God says about Himself or about themselves as His children.

The Core of the Matter

God has explained a great deal about Himself, and about us as His children, in His word. The pervasive doubts so many Christians have about finding (or coming into) God's "good graces" are quite misplaced. There seems to be an undercurrent of insecurity in people as to whether they are pleasing God in their life (and/or worship) and wondering if He accepts their efforts. This is what I mean when I say that the discussion about Jesus' words in John 4 is more about figuring out how to be a person "*the Father seeks to be His worshiper*" than it is about a spiritual and truthful worship. People want to do the worship that will please God so that they will, in turn, know that He accepts them.

Therein lies the problem. God has already spoken to us about this, and His word is firm and unchanging. Yet,

Christians run around trying to do something called "worship" to earn His favor. Has not God called us His children (1 John 3:1)? Has He not declared that we are righteous by faith (Romans 5:1ff), and that Christ joyfully exchanged His righteousness for our sinfulness (2 Corinthians 5:21)? Has He not delivered us from the domain of darkness and transferred us to the Kingdom of His Son (Colossians 1:13)? When God speaks "Christ" into our lives, and we respond by faith, He establishes our salvation—not on the basis of what we have done, or the type of worship we do—but according to His mercy and love (Ephesians 2:8-10; 2 Timothy 1:9-10). When God loves us, there is nothing that can separate us from His love (Romans 9:35-39). God has placed within us a "deposit" of the Holy Spirit that assures us of His complete redemption (Ephesians 1:13-14).

Still, with all of the promises of God clearly expressed and communicated in His word, and the complete assurance His word brings, Christians disbelieve these promises, deny His word, and continue to seek His approval by looking for forms, patterns, and formulas to discover how they might turn His favor toward them. When God says something, and we do not believe it, we essentially are calling Him a liar. Then, when we go out and try to earn His favor on our own, we fall way short. Let us call this for what it is—a sanctification of good works. Paul called the Galatians "fools" for this type of thinking (Galatians 3:1). *"Having begun by the Spirit,"* he writes, *"are you now being perfected by the flesh?"* (Galatians 3:3) These people began by the Spirit and they believed the word about salvation, freely given by God's grace on the basis of faith, without works. Then they immediately turned to good works to try to keep God's favor, in order to be perfected (sanctified) by the flesh.

How foolish it is for us today, as well, to try and figure out how to do the right things to be the one *"the Father seeks."*

The reality is, the Father does not seek you as a result of your worship. He is not moved by what you do or how you do it. He seeks you for one reason and one reason only: His love. His love established a relationship with man at creation, extended mercy at the fall, and restores our relationship to Him in redemption. From beginning to end our relationship with God is dependent upon Him, and any attempt at self-righteousness to gain or retain His favor is foolishness and folly.

True Worshipers

The misunderstanding of this foundational principle of God's grace is at the root of much confusion about worship and the interpretation of John 4:24. Let us consider who the "*true worshipers*" might be that Jesus refers to in John 4:23. Does it not seem obvious that "*in spirit and truth*" are **descriptive** terms rather than terms which designate a pattern, style, or procedure? In other words, the Father seeks and finds true worshipers as they respond to the spirit and truth. This description is a pointer to note that worship is a response of faith, not a response of works (for example, the Samaritan woman in the passage, the "works" consisted of being in the right place). Jesus is not indicating a difference between believers—some of whom worship rightly ("*in spirit and truth*") and others who do not—but **He is describing the difference between believers and unbelievers** in John 4:23-24. It is the response of faith (to God's call in Christ), which allows someone to worship "*in spirit and truth.*" Any other worship is just useless motion.

This passage should be taught as the context teaches, rather than be drawn into a discussion of the legitimacy (or rightness) of a Christian's worship style or form or feeling. There are passages that speak to the judgment of the

Christian, and the judgment of their worship, but this is not one of them. The judgment taking place here is the judgment of faith, or lack thereof. Either a person worships *"in spirit and truth"* as a result of the relationship established by God in making him or her His child, or they worship in "flesh and falsehood" by not responding to God according to His provision and love. This is what the Samaritans were doing, and what Jesus points out to the woman.

In a related passage (just one chapter later in John 5:24-27), Jesus uses similar terminology to describe the difference between the believer and unbeliever. The main connection is Christ's use of the phrase *"an hour is coming, and now is"* which is the same phrase used in John 4. *"Truly, truly, I say to you, an hour is coming and now is, when the dead shall hear the voice of the Son of God; and those who hear shall live"* (John 5:25). It is plain to see that God is the initiator of salvation, and man responds to Him and receives life. In both John chapter 4 and John chapter 5, Christ makes use of the same phrase to begin a short discourse on the difference of true belief and false belief.

Paul reiterates a portion of Christ's words in Philippians 3:3 when he writes, *"for we are the true circumcision, who worship in the Spirit of God and glory in Christ Jesus and put no confidence in the flesh."* This reference, just as Jesus' words, connects salvation with worshiping *"in the Spirit."* Paul is differentiating those who are truly believers, that is those who are circumcised in heart (Romans 2:29; Colossians 2:11-12), with those who are of the "false" circumcision. The unbeliever who is circumcised in the flesh is unredeemed due to a lack of faith, while the believer, through faith in Christ, is truly in a relationship with God and worships in the Spirit. Paul is employing the image of circumcision to recognize those who have a relationship with the true God, just as Israel was recognized as the people of

God in the Old Testament due to the covenant of circumcision (Genesis 17:9-14). True circumcision, and the establishment of a relationship with God, is through faith in Christ.

Christ's View of Worship

In some senses, these observations lead to questions about what Jesus' understanding of worship really was. In other words, when He spoke of worship in John 4, did he really have the intention of relegating it to the internal, limited realm as many modern interpretations suggest? Or, did Jesus have a broader conceptualization of worship similar to what Paul discusses in Romans and Colossians (and other places)?

Let us turn to Christ's own words to piece together an answer for these questions. First, look just a few verses after His conversation with the Samaritan woman. Note the **action** statements within the words of Jesus to describe His mission on earth in John 4:34, *"My food is to do the will of Him who sent Me, and to accomplish His work."* Interesting that this points to a broader purpose for His life than simply an internal communion with God through prayer (such as Zwingli suggested).

Even more telling is His attitude about the Sabbath—the traditional Jewish day of worship. John 5:16 notes that Jesus was being reprimanded and persecuted for performing miracles and good deeds on the Sabbath. His simple reply was one that underscores the value of spiritual **action** (healing) as opposed to some adherence to a code of moral principles (actually a set of rules to show spirituality by a lack of activity!). He says, *"My Father is working until now, and I Myself am working"* (John 5:17).

There are also the statements of John 6:38-40 in which Jesus, again, notes the **activity** for which He came down from heaven: to do God's will, bringing life to those who believe and then restoring them to God. Balanced with this activity are statements of belief and trust. These are definitely inner aspects of faith, but as Paul (Eph 2:10), Peter (1 Peter 1:16ff), and James (James 1) point out to us, the internal belief system must be accompanied by good works showing a faithful and thankful response to God for His work through Christ. The external works express the internal convictions.

Beyond these we find is John 9:4-5 in which Jesus seeks to *"work the works of Him who sent me"* (also similarly in 10:37-38). This is to say nothing of the specific *"purpose"* He mentions in John 12:27, which is the work of the cross. These ideas are underscored again in Jesus' great prayer of John 17 in which he points to His *"finished work"* (vs. 4), how He *"manifested"* God's name (vs. 6, a phrase indicating worship and recognition of God's authority), and that He faithfully passed on God's word to the disciples (vs. 14).

All of these references from the Gospel of John lead us to the same conclusion: ***The type of worship Jesus had in mind was a worship of obedience and of doing the work of God—of being and doing what He came to do***. By successfully reaching his goal, He brought glory (i.e., worship) to His Father. It was both internal through prayer and communion with God, and external in the preaching and works He performed. This was why he came, and He finished His mission. Does this sound familiar? Jesus was doing what He came to do—He was living ***The Heavens Declare Principle***.

No one can deny that Jesus lived a life of worship, and in that life He balanced a steady dose of prayer and communion with His Father, on the one hand, with a busy and productive daily walk among the people, on the other. A life of teaching, healing, doing good, and then teaching some more. This is the pattern of worship: a balance of internal and external factors in a response of obedience to God.

Jesus' words in John 4:23-24 do not refer to worship in our "innerness," but to worship in the power of the Holy Spirit. It is He that empowers our Christian walk. Christ's words do not refer to our version of truth, or some abstract idea of "truth," but to the truth and reality of a personal God revealing Himself in the incarnation of the Son of God.

A Synopsis of Jesus' Ideas on Worship

Geoffrey Wainright, in his systematic theology *Doxology*, gives an excellent synopsis of the thought of Jesus in regards to worship. He points to three features "which Jesus presents for worship understood as human communion with God."[33]

Jesus used 'Abba' to address the Father: "'Abba'...was the word used from child to parent, from disciple to rabbi; it combines intimacy and respect, familiarity and esteem, affection and reverence. Jesus used the word to address *God*. Christians have the same privilege in worship (Romans 8:15f; Galatians 4:6). The word characterizes the whole relationship to which God is calling humanity and which believers already know. The mighty Creator also provides and cares for his creatures with a parent's love; the sovereign Lord wants children, not slaves."[34]

Jesus gave an example of prayer: "The second feature is the Lord's prayer, which is given as a pattern for Christian prayer. It begins with 'Abba', and it brings out, in the fourth, fifth and sixth petitions, the fact that God is the provider, preserver and redeemer of his children. The opening clauses reveal that the glory of God involves the achievement of his will, the coming of

73

his kingdom. For humanity, this *means salvation*; for that is precisely God's intention for mankind. On the human side, the active aspect of salvation is obedience to God: 'Thy will be done'."35

Jesus is obedient: "The third paradigmatic feature of Jesus is, therefore, sacrifice. His obedience to God meant taking up his cross. His self-surrender to God was total. 'Not my will but Thine' was the climactic expression of a life of complete openness to God (Mark 14:36)."36

Rather than focusing primarily on John 4:24 as many authors have done, Wainright shows that Jesus' ideas concerning worship are much more balanced and found throughout his life and teachings. A close interpersonal relationship with the Father as His children (*Abba*), talking and communicating as children to our Father (*prayer*), and following the directives for life given by our loving Father (*obedience*), is a much more balanced perspective on worship as Jesus understood it—and lived it.

Beyond John 4:23-24

In today's "Praise and Worship" over-saturated Christian culture, there appears to be a continued reliance on John 4:23-24 for discussion on worship methods and practice. There is a great need for the Body of Christ, and for its worship leaders and pastors, to go beyond this passage and develop a deeper and broader concept of worship as Jesus lived it and as it is found throughout the whole of Scripture.

God does desire to be pleased by His children, and His children appropriately desire to please Him, as Paul suggests several times (2 Corinthians 5:9; Ephesians 6:6 and others). We must understand, however, that in pleasing the Father we are not endearing ourselves to Him any more than we already are. He loves us. *"We love, because He first loved us"* writes John (1 John 4:19), and no matter what, the process is always in that order: we love, we have faith, we obey because He moves *first* in our lives to love us, draw us near, and guide us in life.

This is the lesson of Christ's full life of worship, and when John 4 is understood in its place within this fuller understanding of worship, we can truly begin to please Him as His children—loved and secure in His care.

Let me close this chapter with some appropriate remarks from A.W. Tozer in his classic treatment of this subject titled *Whatever Happened to Worship?* He reiterates succinctly what has been discussed:

> Men and women continue to try to persuade themselves that there are many forms and ways that seem right in worship. But God in His revelation has told us that He is spirit and those who worship Him must worship Him in spirit and in truth. God takes the matter of worship out of the hands of men and puts it in the hands of the Holy Spirit.
>
> It is impossible for any of us to worship God without the impartation of the Holy Spirit. It is the operation of the Spirit of God within us that enables us to worship God acceptably through that Person we call Jesus Christ, who is Himself God.
>
> So worship originates with God and comes back to us and is reflected from us, as a mirror. God accepts no other kind of worship.[37]

The Judgment of Worship

We have seen that worship is an all-encompassing lifestyle that has qualities that are both internal and external (or spiritual and physical, requiring thought followed by action), and that our worship must be balanced and not swerve into an improper dualism (see comments on Romans 12 in Chapter 1). We have also noted that the individual Christian has been gifted by God to serve others, both believers and unbelievers, and that the *"proper working"* of these spiritual gifts draws together a community which, in turn, worships God as each part functions accordingly (Ephesians 4, Romans 12). Beyond these, we observed that God's creation worships Him by "being and doing what it was created to do" and thus as new creations, Christians also worship primarily by doing what God created them to be and do—by being His children and using their gifts to serve Him and others. This full life of worship is the example of Christ's very life here on earth.

With all of this in mind we must consider the implications of Second Corinthians 5:10, which describes the judgment of believers. I have never found this passage discussed in any book, article, or teaching concerning worship. I do not want to speculate on the reasons for this, but suffice it to say that judgment was not a popular topic in the Church culture of the late Twentieth Century, or now in the Twenty-first Century.

The Context of Paul's Comments

As Paul writes Second Corinthians 5 he is in the midst of a discussion begun earlier about the temporal (that which we see) and the eternal (that which we do not see) (2

Corinthians 4:18ff). As is the regular experience of Christians, Paul is considering the apparent disparity between what we are promised as children of God—life, peace, joy, etc.—and what actually happens to us on a daily basis—death, difficulty, stress, etc.

Let me be clear that Paul is not falling into dualism for, as we discussed in Chapter 1, he avoids it and seeks a balance of the physical and spiritual. A dualistic view would disparage the physical and temporal in order to raise the importance of the spiritual. Paul does not do this at all, and presents a holistic picture. In fact, Paul is directing the reader toward a heightened awareness of physical reality. *"For indeed while we are in this tent,"* by which he means our physical body, *"we groan, being burdened, because we do not want to be unclothed, but to be clothed, in order that what is mortal may be swallowed up by life"* (2 Corinthians 5:4). The indication is that this mortal, physical body we now have will be *"swallowed up"* by a body that is immortal, or eternal. Note that he does not do away with the body, but it is transformed into something beyond what our experience has been up to this point. Our bodies are redeemed and restored to what they were meant to be prior to Adam's sin. He addresses this same issue for the Corinthians in an earlier letter, with the same message (1 Corinthians 15:50-58).

And so, Paul is considering these issues in 2 Corinthians and ultimately comes to the point of judgment, for after death comes judgment for both the believer and unbeliever. Here in this passage, he is dealing with the judgment of the Christian.

The Judgment of the Christian

For we must all appear before the judgment seat of Christ, that each one may be recompensed for his deeds in the body, according to what he has done, whether good or bad. (2 Corinthians 5:10)

Unlike the judgment of the unbeliever, which is based solely on their rejection of Christ as Savior, believers are judged for their deeds—good or bad. Note that this verse specifically says, *"recompensed for his deeds in the body."* The fact that Paul connects this judgment to our **actions** is important in the context of our discussion about worship, for as we have seen, our worship shows itself externally by what we do. This underscores, once again, that worship is holistic, not simply an internal discipline. ***Because this judgment of believers is a judgment of their actions and deeds flowing from internal convictions—it is most directly a judgment of their worship!***

The judgment of Christians at the seat of Christ is a judgment of their actions and deeds in the horizontal level of relationships and life. The believer is judged in accordance with the acting out of his or her faith in the realm of human relationships. It may be called a judgment of our process of sanctification (which can be described as how we live our lives) and our growing and maturing each and every day.

The vertical aspect of our salvation (or our justification before God), on the other hand, is complete and assured. Our relationship to the Father is secured not by what we do, how we do it, when or how often, but only through the work of Christ by His conquering of sin and death. This difference between justification and sanctification shows us that the judgment of believers described in 2 Corinthians 5:10 is based on their sanctification—how they live out their faith in the everyday interaction with others.

The non-believer never makes it to the judgment seat of Christ. The ongoing rupture (as a result of Adam's sin) in his or her relationship with the Father secures his judgment before God. In other words, the judgment of the unbeliever is one of the vertical aspects of salvation, between God and the person, rather than on a horizontal level as for believers. There is no justification for the unbeliever, and thus no salvation. It is not a judgment of the unbeliever's deeds, since no works in and of themselves can re-establish the broken relationship with God (see Romans 3:9-20). The judgment of the unbeliever is determined solely by their rejection of Christ, thus they incur the full punishment for their sins and are condemned to Hell for eternity.

However, once a person becomes justified and responds to God by faith in Christ, he or she enters into another level of judgment. The believer's eternal position is assured, for they have become a child of God and He knows those who are His. Just as there was nothing they could do to gain their salvation, neither is there anything they can do to lose it. It is a work of God, a gift of God. Once a person responds, God calls them His child and He begins the work of sanctification—a setting apart unto holiness and godliness.

Responsibility in Life

Some may read this and think that this becomes a free ride to live any way that they choose because once salvation is secured it will not be taken away. However, my point in this section is to show that with the gift of salvation comes great responsibility. As believers in the process of sanctification, we must *"work out"* our salvation (do good deeds) with *"fear and trembling"* (Philippians 2:12). We do these good deeds not to prove to God that we deserve salvation (because we do not), nor to earn or keep our salvation in any way (because we cannot). Our good deeds are a response of love and thankfulness for what God has done in us. They are the practical extension of the change that took place in the inner man. Again, this is holistic, the inner person and the outer person should come closer to match one another (i.e., the inner man and outer man must have integrity) as the process of sanctification progresses.

These good deeds are opportunities God places in our paths every day, that we may be part of the process of becoming Christ-like, and progressively become the masterpieces He desires. This is what is meant by, *"For we are His workmanship, created in Christ Jesus for good works, which God prepared beforehand, that we should walk in them"* (Ephesians 2:10).

The mutual outworking of good deeds in our lives is a cooperation between what God does in His sovereignty and what we do at our level of responsibility. *"So then, my beloved,"* Paul writes, *"just as you have always obeyed, not as in my presence only, but now much more in my absence, work out your salvation with fear and trembling; for it is God who is at work in you, both to will and to work for His good pleasure"* (Philippians 2:12-13). At one and the same time, we as Christians are completely responsible for working out our salvation and fulfilling the deeds God places before us, **and** God is completely responsible for working in us and bringing us to sanctification. These responsibilities are not contradictory, since God functions and holds responsibility on a different level than man.

We need to become comfortable with this idea and take our responsibility seriously, especially in light of Second Corinthians 5:10. If we worship with our body, mind, spirit, and soul—as a whole person—then the judgment Paul is describing in Second Corinthians is a judgment of our worship. This is the life of worship that we live every day. It is a holistic judgment of our lives, just as worship is a spiritual discipline that covers all that we are and do. This ought to be a sobering thought for those who have not taken the time to consider either their current practices of both public and private worship, or the ramifications of their conduct (i.e., their worship) within the rest of their lifestyle.

Scripture indicates various standards by which our good works will be judged.[38]   First, there is an expectation of quality in what we do for the service of God and others. In First Corinthians 3:1-15, Paul uses the imagery of a fire to describe the judgment of believers. *"Now if any man builds upon the foundation* (the gospel of Christ) *with gold, silver, precious stones, wood, hay, straw, each man's work will become evident...and the fire itself will test the quality of each man's work"* (1 Corinthians 3:12-13). What would our worship be considered?   Will it survive the fire as gold, silver, and precious stones bringing glory to God? Or, will it burn in the flames with the wood, hay, and straw? These are apt figures of speech put to good use to give us vivid pictures of Christ's judgment of believers.

A second expectation in our life of good works is one of faithfulness or responsibility. First Corinthians 4:2 states that *"it is required of stewards that one be found trustworthy."* A steward is a person who is responsible for the household of their master. In the case of the Christian, we are stewards of God's gifts given by the presence of the Spirit, and we are stewards of the Church, which is His body. This means, to be good stewards, we must learn and practice our gifts. We must develop them through mentoring and study. We must put them to use in the service of God and our neighbors (believers and unbelievers) so that our function in the Body of Christ is fulfilled with quality and excellence. This will ultimately help the entire Body of Christ to function properly, which is an expectation for the church (Ephesians 4:11-16).

Third is the area of motivation in our practice of good works. According to First Corinthians 4:5, God will shine a light into our hearts to see our motives as we serve Him, and then *"each man's praise will come to him from God."* This falls right in line with Peter's words uttered after he and the apostles were jailed by the high priests and leaders of the

Jews in Jerusalem (Acts 5:17-32). When commanded to stop preaching Christ, Peter responded, *"We must obey God rather than men"* (vs. 29). He had already made a similar statement to them in Acts 4:19-20, *"Whether it is right in the sight of God to give heed to you rather than to God, you be the judge; for we cannot stop speaking what we have seen and heard."*

Paul also encourages believers to serve,

> *...in the sincerity of your heart, as to Christ; not by way of eyeservice, as men-pleasers, but as slaves of Christ, doing the will of God from the heart. With good will render service, as to the Lord, and not to men, knowing that whatever good thing each one does, this he will receive back from the Lord, whether slave or free.* (Ephesians 6:6-8)

The idea that the Christian will *"receive back from the Lord"* carries connotations of the rewards of judgment and is based upon the motivation of one's heart.

Going Further

To reiterate my point, consider the two prevailing perspectives on the whole idea of "worship." On the one hand, there are those (the majority it seems) that teach, preach, discuss and generally focus on the subject of worship as it relates to the corporate activity. In other words, when we read or hear the word "worship" most often, it is referring to the corporate event of a local congregation, or some derivative form of it (i.e., small groups, concerts, meetings, etc.). The reference to "individual" or "private" worship is generally nominal, and any talk of a worship "lifestyle" inevitably reverts back to the corporate event.

On the other hand, the alternative perspective begins with the overall idea that worship is a lifestyle first—all encompassing and overarching the rest of life. That we come together and worship corporately is, in fact, only a small part of a true picture of "worship" as it seems to be represented in Scripture. Within this grand, foundational picture of worship being all that we are and do, discussions about "corporate" and "private" worship fit seamlessly. This is the perspective that I am presenting here in this book.

Consider this: As the church gathers corporately for "worship" it may be more appropriate to consider it as the primary opportunity for God to communicate Himself to us through His word, the preaching of Christ ("God with us"), and prayer. As we experience His self-revelation we will respond with song and thanksgiving, as we well should, along with many other public expressions. ***Yet our response should not—cannot—stop at the end of the service.***

Our response to God's communicating to us flows out of the "worship service" into our lives. We take His revelation to others in caring for them, serving them and loving those around us. By doing so, we continue our worship activity (remember "*present your bodies*" from Romans 12) as a thankful expression of love to Him.

Some liturgically based churches retain this idea within their own expressions of corporate worship. Unfamiliar to many Western Christians, the Orthodox Church in the Eastern parts of the world draws from a deep well of solid thinking in regards to much of what they do. Note that the terminology is similar to my explanation of God's "initiative" and man's "acknowledgment." Geoffrey Wainright explains,

> The point, in Orthodox terms, is that worship is first and foremost the "presence and act of the Trinitarian God": "Worship is not primarily man's initiative but God's

redeeming act in Christ through His Spirit. The eucharistic sacrifice (i.e., communion or the Lord's Supper) as the center of Christian worship implies the absolute priority of God and his act before man's 'answer' and 'acknowledgment', as we usually describe Christian worship'" (N.A. Nissiotis).[39]

Closer to home, in the Western Church, is this summary of Luther's thought using the terms "divine *beneficium*" or benefit, and man's "response":

> Or, in Lutheran terms: *Gottes-dienst* is God's service to us before it can be our service to God; Luther charged the Roman church with having made the mass a human *sacrificium* directed towards God, whereas the gospel sacrament is a divine *beneficium* directed towards humanity, and our offering of praise and life can only be a response to God's gift.[40]

In either explanation, these ideas give a clearer conceptual framework for worship as a holistic form of life, a thankful response, than simply viewing "worship" as an event—corporate or individual. Certainly these points and the previously considered Scriptures show us the importance of the internal and external aspects of our lives, and therefore reveal the full extent of our worship. I do not believe we should act out of fear in seeking to live a life of worship because it will be judged by Christ. That would be the wrong motivation. I do believe the knowledge of judgment should provoke us to consider our underlying purpose for life, to be responsible with what He has given us, and to serve Him with the best of what we have to offer. When each Christian does this individually, we can then come together and serve as the Body of Christ works properly and completely. This is what God intends from our lives of worship.

Deep and Wide

We have already spent a considerable number of pages examining the Biblical passages that are vital to a balanced understanding of a life of worship. Although I have stated that corporate worship is only a part of the larger conception of worship, it is nevertheless an important part and one that intertwines closely with the larger issues of the life of worship I have been describing.

With that in mind, I think it is appropriate to place this chapter here because of its focus on the ideas of worship. If we are seeking to build a solid foundation and framework for worship then it is right to include this portion of Scripture, even though it broadens into many of the corporate elements that will be discussed later in Part III of this book.

The two somewhat parallel passages in Colossians 3:12-17 and Ephesians 5:18-21 are a transition. They move us from our discussion of the foundational ideas of worship, in the broad sense as a lifestyle of worship, to some considerations of worship in a more public setting. More directly, these passages help the community know how individuals are to minister to one another in a public "worship service." Although a fountain of ideas for the forms and practices of public worship are found in these two passages, there is still a healthy balance between the thought of worship (internal) and the practice of worship (external).

These passages can be considered guidelines and indicators for a balanced approach to worship services as they relate to the community. Too narrow a focus on John 4:24 in recent years, as discussed in Chapter 5, has trapped the discussion of worship in a subjective, self-centered worship that leaves out many important aspects of public worship. Let us here begin to bridge the ideas and framework described in earlier chapters to the actual workings of worship in a church or group setting.

In Colossians 3:12-17 Paul writes,

> *And so, as those who have been chosen of God, holy and beloved, put on a heart of compassion, kindness, humility, gentleness and patience; bearing with one another, and forgiving each other, whoever has a complaint against anyone; just as the Lord forgave you, so also should you. And beyond all these things put on love, which is the perfect bond of unity. And let the peace of Christ rule in your hearts, to which indeed you were called in one body; and be thankful.* **Let the word of Christ richly dwell within you, with all wisdom teaching and admonishing one another with Psalms and hymns and spiritual songs, singing with thankfulness in your hearts to God.** *And whatever you do in word or deed, do all in the name of the Lord Jesus, giving thanks through Him to God the Father.*

The Word of Christ

Let us remember that Paul is writing to primarily small, close-knit house churches filled with people who lived, and worked, and cared for one another in close proximity. The notion of large congregations was not one with which Paul was familiar, and the reality of which did not come about for possibly several hundred years after Paul's lifetime. This makes his admonitions that much more compelling when we read them with that in mind. These Christians knew each other intimately. They observed one another living among their family and friends, in their jobs, and saw how they loved and served other people. The transparency and accountability were significant factors in the life of the New Testament church.

It is also important to note that although verse 16 (the bold-style verse quoted above) is the central thought, the entire context is quoted to show the communal aspects of worship as Paul is expressing them. Being *"chosen of God,"* showing forgiveness and patience, peace and thankfulness, and most importantly demonstrating a unifying love are characteristics that Paul sees as identifiers of a worshiping community. Only after describing these interpersonal and relational aspects of the community does he quickly address a few aspects of a worship service (although, he never actually calls it that).

We might also be attentive to the fact that these verses are directed at the community of believers, rather than the individual believer. Paul is speaking to the collective *"you"* of the church, with obvious implications for the individual. Keeping this in mind will help us to understand the wider ramifications of what he is saying. We have a tendency to read Scripture as though it was directed at us particularly (at "me"), yet as is often the case, the writer is intending to communicate to a group of people (at "us") and how to live life together.

As we look at verse 16, along with the Ephesians passage, the most vital concept encountered is the indwelling of God's word, especially as it is empowered through the presence of the Spirit. Ephesians 5:18-19 says, *"And do not get drunk with wine, for that is dissipation, but be filled with the Spirit, speaking to one another in psalms and hymns and spiritual songs, singing and making melody with your heart to the Lord."* The interpretation of this reference to *"the word of Christ"* should include a broad understanding of its use and can be understood in several ways, each of which has its own significance.

First, the word refers to Christ Himself, as revealed to us in John 1:1 and 14, *"In the beginning was the Word, and the Word was with God and the Word was God...And the Word became flesh, and dwelt among us..."* This reveals an underlying emphasis on Christ in worship for it focuses our worship to be Christocentric. Worship is not about us—how we feel about it, how it "speaks" to us, or even what we have to say to God—worship is about Christ, and in a more encompassing way, about the Trinity. Notice in our passage that the word dwells within the community, like a fountain, from which admonishment, teaching, praise and other elements flow. This is the activity of the Spirit.

Second, the word also refers to Scripture as the word of God. Modern Christians have the tendency to see every reference to "word" as pertaining to Scripture, but a fuller understanding of the term is appropriate in most cases. Here in Colossians there is an obvious connection to Scripture, but the way in which Paul applies the term and connects it with the rest of the context leads one to sense broader implications, as I have already suggested and will continue to suggest. Scripture is God's primary communication of Himself to us, and so it is quite appropriate and Biblical that we should read this reference to "word" as referring to the Biblical text. As Scripture dwells within the community, as God communicates Himself, the community will respond to Him in the various aspects of worship Paul mentions. In a related passage, Paul also encourages Timothy to *"give attention"* to the reading of Scripture and other texts that will help the community through exhortation and teaching (1 Timothy 4:13).

Third, when the word of Christ "dwells" within the community, it often resides in the form of verbal communication between the members of that community. Note that Paul lists some of the forms of this communication in *"teaching and admonishing"* as well as *"singing."* The practice of many churches has been to only hear this verbal communication in the form of preaching or teaching from the pastor (or from the pulpit/podium area of the sanctuary). This does not represent the fullness of what Paul is referring to. Although preaching is one of the forms of God's verbal communication (Luther taught that God's word *must* be preached in order to be heard, from Romans 10:14, "*And how can they hear without a preacher?*"), this passage also indicates that each of the members of the body is to speak these words to every other member (also a concept taught by Luther). In this we see the implications of the priesthood of all believers as Peter teaches in 1 Peter 2:9-10 (and Paul in Romans 15:16), in which believers become intermediaries for one another, bringing the reality of God's grace and forgiveness into each other's lives.

The Purpose

Next in Colossians 3:16 Paul refers to "*teaching and admonishing.*" These are mentioned in the same phrase for a reason. It is not enough to simply teach the fundamental doctrines of the faith without specific and realistic guidance as to how these doctrines should affect the daily walk of faith. At the same time, giving moral and ethical advice in the form of admonishment is groundless without a solid foundation of doctrinal and theological teaching upon which to establish those guidelines. We must teach and admonish in balance. "We can talk about methods," writes Schaeffer, "we can stir each other up, we can call each other to all kinds of action, but unless it is rooted in a strong Christian base in the area of content and the practice of truth, we build on sand and add to the confusion of our day."[41]

Not only must we teach and admonish in balance, but also with variety. The variety that Paul establishes with the phrase "*with Psalms and hymns and spiritual songs*" is vague for a reason: he has just spent a significant portion of chapter two of Colossians discussing, and warning against, the establishment of human traditions that would supersede the ordinances of God.

Although we know that Paul adopts the term *"Psalms"* to refer to the Old Testament book of Psalms, it is unclear what he means by the two terms *"hymns"* and *"spiritual songs."* Some have suggested, and even taught as fact, that *"hymns"* refer to some kind of doctrinal or theologically impregnated song and that *"spiritual songs"* refer to a person's responsive, personalized song *"from the heart"* (cf. Ephesians 5:19). There is, however, no Scriptural or historical evidence that these definitions are true or that they are what Paul meant by describing them as he did. In fact, many scholars maintain that Paul meant to be purposely vague. By doing so, he avoids setting up a new system of traditions in place of the ones he just condemned earlier in Colossians, while allowing for a diversity that can flex within culture and time.

Variety and Balance

With reference to variety, and redemption of the arts in particular, Jeremy Begbie writes, "The musician's calling, as with any creative artist, is to discover, respect, and develop what he or she has received in creation, and to form out of the disorder of the world a richer order."[42] Within the walls of the church creativity and innovation should abound as we bring the word of God in all of its forms to all who need to hear it.

We have inherited the broadest views on the use of music in worship from Martin Luther. I have already spent some time showing the limited and narrowing ideas of John Calvin and Ulrich Zwingli, but I did not at that time give a clearer sense of Luther's views. For Luther, church music had a three-fold purpose:

- the praise of God;
- an offering of the congregation; and
- Christian education of humanity.[43]

In general, Luther allowed music of all kinds to be an integral part of church life. For him, it was another tool to be used in the teaching of the word of God. "I am willing," he said, "to make German Psalms for the people, after the example of the prophets and the ancient fathers; that is, spiritual hymns whereby the Word of God, through singing, may conserve itself among the people."[44]

I find it interesting that Paul clearly indicates that music is to be utilized for "*teaching and admonishing*" as well as "*singing with thankfulness*" to God. These are broad and sweeping responsibilities for the use of music within the church. Yet, many churches remain in the paradigm that the sermon is the primary form of "*teaching and admonishing*." In fact, churches regularly (and too narrowly) focus music only upon an upward "me to God" dynamic of what they narrowly call "worship." Paul, on the other hand, sets the stage for a broad variety and underlying diversity in teaching and admonishing through music. A broader discussion of this is found in Chapter 12.

On a side note, these ideas further establish the need, in our time, for theologically trained and competent pastors whose roles are to care for the music programs in the church. The fact that most churches allow musicians to lead their congregations in this area unwittingly places a person into a pastoral role without the benefit of pastoral training or a pastoral call. I am not suggesting that these musicians are not gifted or even that they are not good leaders. Some may even have wonderful people skills. What I am saying is that in Colossians, and in other places, Scripture clearly identifies these musical aspects of worship as integral in the teaching ministry of the church. If they are so, then it can only benefit the church that leaders of worship ministries are as highly trained in theology as they are in music. (By the way, this also means that a trained pastor should have a significant background in music to lead these areas as well!!) I will deal with these issues more fully in Chapter 15.

In verse 17, Paul underscores the balance of what we have already seen about worship in other passages; that it is something that fully encompasses all that we are. He says *"in word and deed."* Both the inner world of the thoughts, mind and emotions as well as the outer world of the senses, physical work, and good deeds is to be done in Christ's name, with thankfulness to God. This is worship with our whole being. Worship done in balance.

Part II: The Life of Worship

I hope it has now become apparent that the basis for a solid understanding of the broad concept of worship is Scripture. Once that base is built it can become a foundation and framework for building an unlimited diversity of structures, and we shall see that diversity is part of the plan.

Although the concept of worship is totally interrelated when discussing individual and/or corporate worship, we can learn a great deal about either of the two by considering them independently of each other. You will notice that though we may attempt to discuss them independently, they are truly and completely dependent upon and intertwined with each other. Corporate worship flows from individual worship, and individual worship takes place within the community of believers.

We now come to the second part of our consideration of worship, and that is to consider some specifics of worship as a lifestyle. As I have noted numerous times, there must be a congruency between what is internal and what is external. There must be a direct connection with what the Scriptures say about worship to what we believe about worship to what we do about worship. And that is what this next section of this book is about.

I am purposely placing this section prior to the consideration of corporate worship for several reasons. The main reason is that the paradigm I am seeking to build begins with a Biblical and theological foundation and flows out from there into life. I think it is clear that worship flows into our personal lives first, and then into the corporate life of the church. Another reason I choose to put it first is that the life of worship is all encompassing, and corporate worship is a part of that larger picture. I also feel that by overemphasizing the discussion of worship into a corporate realm has disconnected the reality of worship in everyday life. Dealing with the life of worship first simply makes sense.

There are many ways that this can be presented, and I would like to look at four areas, or four facets, of our Christian life that seem to come together in this concept of worship as a lifestyle. The Scripture passages cited in the following chapters indicate the connections, and the interplay of the thoughts allows these four ideas to flow together well.

First, we will consider some of the specifics of *"renewing the mind."* This has been identified already as one of the most important aspects of worship and the Christian life.

Second, the whole area of spiritual giftedness will be approached. As we will see, this is where diversity in unity flourishes and how the Body of Christ can become all that God intended for it to be.

Third, when all is said and done, the Christian life—the life of worship—is a life of love and service. It is service to God. It is service to our neighbor: our families, our fellow Christians, our friends, and co-workers.

Fourth, and finally, we will draw all this together and attempt a balanced perspective for living a life of worship that keeps the proper perspective of each area discussed.

Ultimately, this will lead us to the third major part of our book, which will be considerations and implications of all these ideas for corporate worship. But, first things first...

Renewing the Mind

Given the approach in these pages of broadening the understanding of worship into a fuller discussion of the daily Christian life, it is appropriate to specifically consider some of the issues regarding this everyday life. As noted repeatedly, *our thinking and theological understanding about worship is the beginning point of our ability to live a Christian life of worship.*

In a sense, the structure of the book itself is an example of this. By beginning our discussion with laying a framework, or foundation, of Scripture and ideas, we now can begin to build upon that framework in varied and unlimited ways. Of course, knowledge is not enough if it does not flow out of our minds and hearts into the world and lives of people around us.

Let us take some time now and consider the admonishment Paul gives that comes on the heels of presenting our bodies as a *"spiritual service of worship."* Romans 12:2 states,

> *And do not be conformed to this world, but be transformed by the renewing of your mind, that you may prove what the will of God is, that which is good and acceptable and perfect.*

The admonishment is apparently two-fold, that is, Paul warns us to *"not be conformed"* to the world around us (remember, that is a reference to the influence of our culture and the world system), and also instructs us to be *"transformed by the renewing of your mind."* In the end, the "goal" for us is to understand and know the will of God.

To clarify, Paul is giving the image, or a model, for the balanced Christian lifestyle in Romans 12:1-2. The elements of this balance of a spiritual worship are:

- that it comes through God's mercy and grace,
- that it is physical (external) in the use of our bodies,
- that it is mental (internal) as our minds are transformed, and
- that it results in a life pleasing and acceptable to God.

So within the balanced life, our whole being is to be part of the worship of God.

The hinge point still remains part of the internal aspect of the mind. The whole principle of balance as it is presented seems to turn on the idea of *"renewing the mind"* that it may be ***transformed*** into something that it is not by nature. To be reminded, once again, by Schaeffer, "We can say two things about the external act: the external follows the internal, and the external is a product of the internal. Thoughts are first, and they produce the external. This is the order."[45] This being the case, we must spend some time considering what it means to *"renew the mind"* in order to be transformed.

"Do not be Conformed"

Along with Romans 12:2, the concept of *"renewing the mind"* appears in Ephesians 4:22-24 which brings further clarification of what Paul meant by, *"do not be conformed to the world."* It reads:

> *...that in reference to your former manner of life, you lay aside the old self, which is being corrupted in*

accordance with the lusts of deceit, and that you be renewed in the spirit of your mind, and put on the new self, which in the likeness of God has been created in righteousness and holiness of the truth.

We can see here that Paul's idea is the same as in Romans 12, but he has adopted different terminology. In Romans he said, *"do not be conformed to this world,"* whereas here in Ephesians he uses a specific image of what that means. He encourages the believer to *"lay aside the old self"* which represents the *"former manner of life."* In other words, believers live a certain way before they come to know Christ, and after they meet Him things are to be different. In some ways, however, this is not automatic. The daily life of a Christian becomes a matter of daily choices to live a life that is in accordance with God's purposes and will. As Jesus said, *"If anyone wishes to come after Me, let him deny himself, and take up his cross daily, and follow me"* (Luke 9:27).

And so what does it mean to not *"be conformed"* or to *"lay aside the old self,"* or in Jesus' words, *"deny"* oneself? Paul indicates the meaning of this and how we might identify and eliminate these influences from our lives when he uses the phrases *"former manner of life"* and *"corrupted in accordance with the lusts of deceit."*

The life of the unbeliever is a selfish one. When Isaiah describes the human predicament, he acknowledges, *"All of us like sheep have gone astray, each of us has turned to his own way"* (Isaiah 53:6). When we turn our own way, it is always **away** from God. That is what the sin of Adam has placed in each of us who are human. We are by nature, as a result of that original sin, selfish and self-seeking. Even the "good" acts we might do as an unbeliever are considered *"filthy garments"* (Isaiah 64:6) in the eyes of God and these works can by no means make us right with Him.

The Psalmist, as quoted by Paul, writes, *"There is none righteous, not even one; there is none who understands, there is none who seeks for God; All have turned aside, together they have become useless; there is no one who does good, there is not even one"* (Romans 3:10-11 quoting Psalm 14). Paul's conclusion from these statements is that all people, whether Jew or Greek (for Paul this designation included every nation and people on earth) are under sin.

The very first step, then, is to move from this life of turning **away** from God to one in which we can turn **toward** Him. This is called salvation, and only comes as a free gift of God through the work of Christ on the cross. As the passages quoted above clearly state, we have no righteousness (i.e., goodness that will bring us into a good standing with God) of our own. Yet, God can only accept into His presence those who are righteous in His eyes.

Thankfully, God provided a way for us in His Son. Second Corinthians 5:21 refers to this in a beautiful way, *"He made Him who knew no sin to be sin on our behalf, that we might become the righteousness of God in Him."* Jesus lived a perfect life, with no sin, and within His person carried pure righteousness. He then offered His life, in submission and obedience to the Father, and took our sin upon Himself. He gave us His righteousness. He exchanged places with us so that we might have a relationship with the Father. This is truly a joyous exchange: Christ for our sins, and His righteousness for us!

This new relationship with God, provided as a gift through Christ, now puts us on the other side of the line, so-to-speak. Paul says, *"Therefore if any man is in Christ, he is a new creature; the old things passed away, behold, new things have come"* (2 Corinthians 5:17). This parallels the *"new self"* and *"old self"* language found in Ephesians 4.

Further Steps to *"Not Conform"*

Once an individual has come through the first step into the free gift of salvation, and is in a place as a believer in which the *"new self"* is present, Paul instructs them to get to work. Philippians 2:12-13 tells us that we are to *"work out"* our own salvation and that *"God is at work"* in us to bring us to maturity. Our balanced Christian life, a life of worship, grows as we work hand-in-hand with God. He does not leave the entire responsibility on us any more than we can expect Him to work out all the details of life without our involvement. It is a relationship and must operate at both levels.

To understand what Paul means when he says, *"do not be conformed to this world,"* we must understand the "world" he is referring to. In other words, what exactly does he mean by *"the lusts of deceit"* that we are to separate ourselves from? How can we identify those specific things that would cause us to turn and walk away from Him?

John gives us a good indication when he writes, *"For all that is in the world, the lust of the flesh and the lust of the eyes and the boastful pride of life, is not from the Father, but is from the world"* (1 John 2:16). We can examine each of these a little further to help us identify them in our own lives. We must daily and actively seek to stem the tide of desire that continues to reside within us, even after salvation. This is the damage sin has caused, but the Lord has provided tools with which we can combat the effects of sin in our lives.

The *"lust of the flesh"* is that set of desires and cravings that cause us to selfishly provide for our own wants. The flesh is a powerful inner voice, part of the nature of man that seeks our own "good" in spite of the needs or wants of those around us. From this flows abuse of every kind, and damaged, hurtful relationships. The cry of self-sufficiency is the cry of the lust of the flesh, thinking that if we gather everything that meets our needs, wants, and desires we will have need of nothing, and no one, else.

The *"lust of the eyes"* is the vision that fuels our own self-sufficiency. We see what others have: beautiful houses, beautiful cars, beautiful women or men, huge bank accounts. Then we begin to envy. We desire those things whether we have earned them or deserve them. This form of lust convinces us that we deserve what we see because it is available around us. The cry of deservedness is the cry of the lust of the eyes: we deserve it because we can obtain it.

The *"boastful pride of life"* is the resulting pride from the fulfillment of all we crave. Once we become self-sufficient and can attain anything we desire, we imagine that we are important because of "all I have accomplished." The cry of attention ("Look at me!") and adoration is the cry of the pride of life: we want others to feel as good about us as we do about ourselves and our accomplishments.

If you want to see a list of specific activities that might represent what this looks like, refer once again to Ephesians 4 and look just prior to the verses we have already discussed. Paul describes those involved in this kind of life this way: *"They have become callous, [and] have given themselves over to sensuality, for the practice of every kind of impurity with greediness"* (4:19). If you were to glance back to Chapter 2 of this book, you will find some incredible similarities between this statement and what we discovered in Romans 1.

Paul also gives a longer description in Galatians 5:16-21,

> *But I say, walk by the Spirit, and you will not carry out the desire of the flesh. For the flesh sets its desire against the Spirit, and the Spirit against the flesh; for these are in opposition to one another, so that you*

may not do the things that you please. But if you are led by the Spirit, you are not under the Law.
Now the deeds of the flesh are evident, which are: immorality, impurity, sensuality, idolatry, sorcery, enmities, strife, jealousy, outbursts of anger, disputes, dissensions, factions, envying, drunkenness, carousing, and things like these, of which I forewarn you just as I have forewarned you that those who practice such things shall not inherit the kingdom of God.

Paul describes the *"deeds of the flesh"* arising from a life being lived *"according to the flesh."* When we see these tendencies in ourselves—and do not fool yourself into thinking they are not there—we are recognizing the influence of the world in our lives. We must take steps to halt the progress and follow the path of righteousness and holiness. In the midst of a culture that glories in lust, pride, and materialism, this is hard work. But God has given us tools, and the inner working of His Spirit, to combat this influence in our lives if we are willing to put our hand to the plow.

Transforming the Mind

The discussion above is quite negative in some senses. It tells us what **not** to do, what activities **not** to be involved with, and the like. For centuries the Christian church has often been stuck at this juncture and has given lists of rules for the people to follow. Although presented most often as a list of "do's" and "don'ts" the lists were more often than not a list of "don'ts." In this section I would like to consider the other side of the list. This is done in pursuit of a balanced perspective.

As expressed in Romans 12, Paul wants us to *"renew our minds"* so that we are transformed. We are all influenced by the world as described above, yet Paul gives detailed steps for being "transformed" into something else. He wants us to be transformed into a person who glorifies God (worships) in every area of life, every day, with every decision. It is a process, it takes work, but it is possible to grow daily in that direction.

So what does *"renewing the mind"* exactly look like? How does it happen? What do we need to do to be sure that it happens on a daily basis? Paul's words in Galatians 5:16 are, *"But I say, walk by the Spirit, and you will not carry out the desire of the flesh."* And what, specifically, does it mean to walk by the Spirit? How do I do that? How do I know if I am walking by the Spirit and not by the flesh?

All of these are good questions, and ones that Christians have been asking for centuries. Let me share some ideas with you, recognizing that this is a process that grows and expands as a believer matures in his or her faith. There are many other books and courses written to help and encourage us toward a greater spiritual walk and dependency upon God, and I recommend several in Appendix A. These points below seem to me to be the most essential for thinking correctly about our Christian life, and ultimately about living a life of worship.

The first, foremost, and absolutely essential element in "renewing the mind" is regular reading, studying and living by the guidelines set forth in the Bible. The Bible is the cornerstone of our faith, and without a daily commitment and re-commitment to pursue God as He reveals Himself through Scripture, we will get sidetracked and distracted. Remember that this is the primary way that God teaches us about Himself, our redemption in Christ, and how we might love and serve Him in a way that honors Him. It is also how He teaches us about ourselves as His children and how to keep perspective in life.

There are probably as many ways to study the Bible, as there are believers. This is simply diversity, and it really ought not be threatening. When one believer describes his or her own method of devotional reading or serious study, we should be encouraged to pursue the same commitment, but not necessarily copy their methods. The importance lies not in how we study, or what method of study we choose, but that we are studying and growing and learning.

Do not assume by my words, however, that I am promoting a "me and the Bible" mentality that allows each person to interpret Scripture as he or she sees fit. There are certain aspects of Bible study that we must adhere to in order to know that what we believe about what we are reading and studying is actually what God meant for us to learn. We do not live our lives in a vacuum, nor do we study Scripture in anonymity. There are believers throughout the centuries who have studied and written concerning every aspect of Biblical study, and we should be willing to learn from them and listen to their wisdom. As I heard recently, "No one knows everything about anything." We will need help along the way. Learning Scripture is meant to take place within the community of believers—the Church, the Body of Christ.

So, here are some elements of allowing God's word to "renew" our minds. First, simply read the Bible from beginning to end. I am still surprised at my own theological upbringing and training that I was never required to read the Bible in its entirety from beginning to the end. Never. In fact, I became an ordained pastor without ever reading through the book completely. I do not mean to place any blame, I just wonder how I missed it. Now, thankfully, through some well-placed encouragement of some respected individuals, I have read through several times—and it has changed my perception of theology and God's redemptive activity.

A complete reading of Scripture gives a glimpse of the "big picture." There is some evidence that the whole Bible rests upon a good understanding of what God was doing in the first five books known as the Pentateuch, also called the Books of Moses. If all we have ever done is read the Gospels, some of the epistles, and a few of the Psalms, we are missing quite a bit of the story.

I would encourage you to begin today. Open to Genesis 1:1 and just start. Read as much as you can each day. It may take several months or a year to finish, but it will be worthwhile and beneficial in your walk with God.

Beyond a complete reading of Scripture, one must also take the time to be in a disciplined pattern of devotional reading and prayerful response. What I mean by this is the opportunity to read some portion of Scripture, meditate on it, and prayerfully consider what God is teaching about Himself, yourself, and the world around you. Sometimes you will even come across prayers that are an integral part of the passage you're reading. For example, Philippians 1:9-11 is such a prayer and reads:

> *And this I pray, that your love may abound still more and more in real knowledge and all discernment, so that you may approve the things that are excellent, in order to be sincere and blameless until the day of Christ; having been filled with the fruit of righteousness which comes through Jesus Christ, to the glory and praise of God.*

Now that I type those verses and read them once again, I realize what a great synopsis they are in describing a life of worship. It is the balanced life of love, powered by knowledge and discernment of God and the work of Christ. This results in the worship of God. Amazing! Imagine praying this prayer for yourself, for your spouse, for your children, for your pastor, for the elders of the church, for missionaries around the world. Think of what the reality of these few verses are, and then realize Scripture is full of this—and God wants our lives to be transformed by such knowledge through the renewing of our minds!

These types of biblical prayers can be used to pray for yourself and others, but also serve to help us pray Scripture from passages that are not necessarily "prayers" in and of themselves. By reading Scripture, meditating on its lessons, and praying through those lessons we will allow God to speak directly to us and mold our thinking to His thinking. That is the transformation that takes place, which is what *"renewing the mind"* means. He wants us to think rightly about life, love, and others.

Going Deeper

We should also take some time to study Scripture at greater depth. There are many useful ways that this can be worked into our lives. Many people seem to respond well to prepared manuals that guide the reader through the study of a passage, book, or doctrine. This can be accomplished individually, but is often more fruitful when done in a group study. A small group will provide accountability as well as opportunities for discussion. One might also look into taking a class at a local Bible college, if time and finances are available to do so.

By engaging in an in-depth study, we begin to open ourselves not only to the valuable input of others, but also the skillful and educated input of scholars and pastors. We will find that many of the study guides available in the marketplace have been prepared by experts in the fields of Old Testament or New Testament studies, professors at Christian colleges and universities, or pastors whose ministries show great fruit.

Beyond these modern resources, we must also look into our past. Christian doctrine—those beliefs that we hold as vital to the Christian faith—were forged out of discussion that sometimes lasted several decades. In the early centuries of the Christian church, what we today take for granted as the central tenets of faith (the doctrine of the Trinity is one example), was defined, redefined, challenged and crafted over years of debate and consideration. It is vital for us to remain connected to these discussions and the thought processes behind them.

We can remain "connected" to Christian Church history by supplementing our study of Scripture with the study of the ecumenical creeds, specifically the Apostles' Creed, the Nicene Creed and the Athanasian Creed. When we begin to unfold the rich history and thought of these documents, we establish a continuity with those who have come before us, and we pass on these truths to those who will come after us. This continuity helps us keep perspective on the broader concept of the Body of Christ. The Creeds also contain short, memorable phrases that give a synopsis of all we hold dear. I have included these three Creeds in Appendix B.

We also can refer to some of the great catechisms of our faith. A catechism was a form of teaching that sought to bring a believer through the various important doctrines of faith and help establish a belief that was consistent with Scripture and Christian history. Most of these are directly related to specific denominations or groups, and when brought alongside the Creeds mentioned above they can be powerful tools to grow and learn the Christian faith.

Although the modern church has strayed far from the practice, in the beginning centuries those wishing to become members of the church (called "catechumens") were not only required to study, know and defend Christian doctrine (the "catechism"), but they also were subject to a close scrutiny of their daily lives. Often this observation of their lives by the elders and bishops went on for months or even years. Think of trying that next time someone wants to join your church!

At another level we can consult Biblical commentaries and writings on theology that will help us learn how to interpret Scripture. There are a multitude of these out there and I would encourage you to approach your pastor or local Bible professor to suggest reliable authors for your consideration. Just because it is in print does not mean it is necessarily a good piece of scholarship.

It is important to see the progression here and remember that Scripture is the ultimate authority that establishes the truth of a Creed, Catechism, commentary, sermon, radio or TV program, or any other way in which someone claims to speak on God's behalf. That is why James tells us that teachers within the Body of Christ will incur a *"stricter judgment"* than others (James 3:1). The teacher, preacher, writer is representing God—and that is serious business!

Moving from "Knowing" to "Doing"

As we allow the Spirit of God to transform us by the *"renewing of our minds,"* and we keep Scripture in front of us on a daily basis, we will begin to see the necessity of actually doing the things, and living the life, that God is expecting of us. No longer can we read a verse and allow its meaning to slip by unnoticed; we must begin to change the way we act. Why? Because our inner mind is changing. Only by changing the mind first can we then alter (in a right way) the things that we do. This is what Paul calls living *"by the Spirit"* in Galatians 6.

Second Timothy 3:16 establishes a sort of progression in this matter of our inner life changing the patterns of the outer life. Paul is sharing with Timothy the importance of the wisdom found in the Scriptures, and that a life based upon the principles found there will grow and mature. *"All*

Scripture," writes Paul, "*is inspired by God and profitable for teaching, for reproof, for correction, for training in righteousness, that the man of God may be adequate, equipped for every good work.*"

Notice that the beginning of the process is the Scriptures, and the end of the process is good works. This is no mistake, and remains consistent with what we have seen before. A truly spiritual and Christian life, one that wholly seeks to worship God in all that we do, is a life that is active **externally** and supported by a foundation of solid theological and Biblical thinking **internally**.

I mentioned the "progression" that is evident in this passage. The focus on Scripture indicated here is the same focus I presented in the previous two sections of this chapter, and this focus is profitable to us. Here we find out why it is profitable: for teaching, for reproof, for correction and for training in righteousness. Let me paraphrase this a bit for clarification.

When we study Scripture, it profits us because it is **teaching** us. In other words, we are learning what God reveals of Himself and how we are to live. What we learn is profitable, as well, for **reproof.** Think of it this way: what we learn of God's principles will begin to convict us of a need to change and conform to these principles. This leads to the next aspect of profit, in that we receive **correction**. Suffice it to say that at this point we have learned what God says, been convicted of our own inadequacies, and now replace our previous thoughts with those that are consistent with Scripture.

So the pattern is like this: We learn, we are convicted, we correct our thinking. This is the internal pattern of "*renewing the mind.*" This ultimately leads to the final part of how Scripture profits us by what is called "*training in righteousness.*" This training is more than just internal, and now takes us into the external realm of good works.

Training in righteousness is that which helps us take what we know internally and express it, or show it, externally. In Paul's words we are *"equipped for every good work."*

By walking through this process on a daily basis, our minds will be renewed and we will learn to walk in the power of the Holy Spirit. When this happens, then we will know that we can avoid carrying out *"the desire of the flesh"* that Paul warns us about. It takes commitment and it takes discipline, but God's word tells us that it can happen.

An Example

Let us consider an example of how significant a renewed mind can become in a life of worship. In Philippians 4:8-9 Paul gives a short description of how to implement one aspect, or method, of *"renewing the mind"* so that we can be transformed into the new man (or woman) God desires us to be:

> *Finally, brethren, whatever is true, whatever is honorable, whatever is right, whatever is pure, whatever is lovely, whatever is of good repute, if there is any excellence and if anything worthy of praise, let your mind dwell on these things. The things you have learned and received and heard and seen in me, practice these things; and the God of peace shall be with you.*

I would like to describe these verses as a kind of filter that we should use to pass through many of our decisions in life. The fibers of the filter are the list of very positive and God-honoring thoughts. Think of it in the same way as a coffee filter which filters out the grounds and allows the liquid to pass through. These verses can act the same way as we view the world around us. By the way, this is what "worldview" is all about.

The phrase *"let your mind dwell on these things"* is key to implementing this method. The concept of "dwelling" on something is to spend time thinking about it and considering the implications of it in life. To think about truth, for instance, is to meditate about *what* is true, *why* it is true, what it *means* in my life for truth to be present, and how that should *change* my thinking and behavior in response to truth. And these are broad principles. Surely all truth is God's truth, and assuming that we can only find it in Scripture is quite shortsighted. But this is only one aspect of the idea of dwelling or thinking on these virtues.

This list also gives us criteria for deciding how to spend our time and our money in relation to the entertainment we choose, the friends we associate with, and the activities we involve ourselves in. These are real life choices that present themselves on a daily basis. When we read that we are to think on *"whatever is lovely"* and allow our minds to dwell on the lovely and the beautiful, what does that mean in the context of the video games that we, or our children, are playing for entertainment purposes? All too often we hear of the unfortunate relationship between a person's unlawful actions and their previous time spent with violent video games. This is part of what the Columbine shootings, and other tragedies, have taught us, yet since then violent video games are more popular than ever and more and more kids (and adults) are playing them. For the Christian who is to think about and dwell upon the lovely and the pure, violence for entertainment purposes is a highly questionable and troublesome habit.

What about the movies filled with violence and explicit sexual scenes? What about the books we read, the magazines we read, our attitudes toward money and possessions, our views about race and social problems? In one way or another we can pass these things through the "filter" of Philippians 4:8-9 and allow God to teach us, renew our minds, and help us to find a truly Christ-like response to our world around us. This can happen every day!!

I believe entertainment choices to be the greatest downfall of the Christian Church in our lifetime. If we were to filter our entertainment choices based on this list, how would that change the movies we watch, the music we listen to, and the books or magazines we read? The stuff of modern media entertainment is filled with impurity, lust, sexual deviancy, violence, questionable morals, and the praise of individuals with grave character flaws. Yet on any Sunday morning, in many churches, we can hear conversations about the latest movie, the latest fad, the best new music idol, or any number of cultural idiosyncrasies.

Granted, we must be aware of our culture—its high points and its faults—and respond to it through a well-grounded Christian worldview. What is inappropriate is the submersion by Christians into cultural norms that may violate Biblical standards of thought and conduct. This ought not to be the case. The Christian life ought to look different. Being aware of the culture and being able to discern the underlying worldview it represents can only come after a person has spent considerable time in *"renewing the mind"* with Scripture and the truth of God. Unfortunately, many Christians are ill-prepared to properly think through the implications of what the culture around them means.

By simply using Philippians 4:8-9 as a filter to daily make choices on what to think about and let our minds dwell on—and what not to think about, or at least seek to avoid—our minds would be renewed and our lives transformed. This is not some pie-in-the-sky idea that is only for the super-saint. Paul views this within the attainment of every believer. Think how liberating it would be to have your mind filled most of the time with truth, honor, purity and excellence. This can happen, if you are willing to work at it and make decisions consistent with what Paul is teaching.

The Target

I would like to share a diagram with you that has proven quite engaging in teaching these concepts, especially as we seek to have our external actions match our inner belief systems. The diagram is based upon a simple target: a series of concentric circles of four or five layers. I have found this diagram to be beneficial for believers of all ages, and accessible to children as young as four years old.

We will work from the center of the diagram and describe what we find in each circle.

First, "The Core" represents the Bible and orthodox Christian doctrine. This area is not in our control, and is the realm of God the Father, Son and Holy Spirit. God has established this core of faith upon the reality and force of His word.

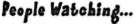

The second circle represents our "Values." We might ask, "WHY do we do what we do?" We begin to determine why we respond to the world around us based on what God has revealed at the core of our belief system.

The next circle moves into the area of our "Priorities." We might ask, "HOW will we do our VALUES?" We cannot do everything, or meet absolutely everyone's needs, so we must prioritize based upon our values, which in turn are based upon the core established by God. It is in our Priorities that we begin seeing the internal become external in regards to planning, and that builds right to the next level.

Fourth, we find the circle of "Goals." We might ask ourselves, "WHAT will we do to show our PRIORITIES?" We really begin to put external plans and strategies together to match the internal VALUES and PRIORITIES that we have determined based upon God's core of the faith.

Finally, we come to the outer circle of "Action." It is here that we ask, "WHEN will we do our GOALS?" The rubber meets the road at this point and the internal elements should now show in the external arena of life. The ultimate goal is for our outer circle of "Action" to match the internal "Core" of God's word.

You will notice that each circle builds upon the previous. This is absolutely critical, and if something breaks down in the flow from one circle to the next, then the external will not properly manifest the internal. Take anything you are a part of, any decision that must be made, any ministry you participate in, or anything else and apply this model. It will be enlightening and challenging to be sure. This can be done on a personal basis, in your family, or with any organization.

And, for the kicker, there are people watching you, but all that they can see is the outer circle. They see your actions. If they hear your words of faith, but see a life of unfaith, they will notice. If they understand the importance of love in the life of a Christian, but see a lack of love in your life, they will wonder. If people discern the inconsistency in the flow from one circle to the next, they will not be convinced that what you say you believe is really what you believe for every day life. Maybe on Sunday, but not the rest of the week.

Conversely, people will take special notice of a life that is truly devoted to Christ. As love flows out of a life in thankfulness to God, resulting in care and service toward others, the lesson of the target will be fully operational. The outer ring of your actions will speak loudly of the core convictions that lie deep within your faith.

"It's not Easy being Green"

Kermit the Frog, in his own unique way, sings of the woes of ordinary life of a frog in the song, *"It's not Easy Being Green."* Green-ness is normal for the frog, but apparently that does not make life any easier. It can sometimes feel the same way with us as Christians. I hope no one has ever been promised a life of ease and comfort as a Christian. There will be joy, but sometimes through hardship and trouble. Real, daily Christianity is often difficult and requires an ongoing commitment to do what God says. We battle a subtle foe. I hope you have seen by now that it is not enough to just *say* you believe it, yet that is as far as many Christians ever get.

It is only by continually identifying those areas that must come under Christ's Lordship and actively working to bring them to His feet that we will find victory in our daily Christian life. We must see the world and its lusts for the spiritual trap that they are, learn the patterns of life and methods from Scripture that give us a solid foundation for a spiritual life, and then actually put those methods into practice every day, day after day. ***This is the true life of worship: it begins by the internal renewal of the mind and grows outward into the total transformation of our lives.***

As God works in us and we cooperate with Him, the process of maturing and growing will lead to greater fulfillment for ourselves and those that we serve. *"Consider it all joy, my brethren,"* James writes, *"when you encounter various trials, knowing that the testing of your faith produces endurance. And let endurance have its perfect result, that you may be perfect and complete, lacking in nothing"* (James 1:2-4). This is the ultimate goal God has established for us, that we might be *"perfect and complete, lacking in nothing."* These are words of victory. These are words of wholeness. These are the words of God's promise: that He desires us to become all that He meant us to be.

Your Spiritual Gifts

I have referred often in these pages to the gifts God has given to each member of the Body of Christ and how the use of these gifts represents a large portion of what, in the broadest sense of the term, we can call a life of worship. It is appropriate, then, to at least spend a few pages discussing this specific doctrine of spiritual gifts and their use in more detail.

No attempt is being made to cover this subject in its entirety. Many books have been written covering spiritual gifts, and courses are available to help a person discover, develop, refine, and use their gifts in ways that both honor God and serve the church. I have taught a course in which twelve to sixteen weeks are spent just learning about and beginning the process of discovery and use of gifts. I make several recommendations for further study in Appendix A, and suggest a review of those materials if you seek more information on this subject.

In synopsis, let me at least review several points, which I believe to be at the center of the spiritual gifts issue. First, I would like to deal with the primary Biblical passages concerning the gifts and their use. Then I will give an outline describing how a person might discover and develop their gifts. Finally, I give some pointers on how someone might refine and focus their gifts and continue to serve God and the Body of Christ faithfully with them.

The Main Passages and General Principles

There are four main passages in the New Testament that cover the subject of spiritual gifts. By far the most revealing and detailed is First Corinthians 12. Beyond that we have already seen that Romans 12 incorporates this element of giftedness, as does Ephesians 4. This rounds out Paul's primary discussions of gifts. Peter lends his voice in First Peter 4. Other than passing references in other places, these give the majority of the detail for the subject.

Although each of these four passages contains a "list" of spiritual gifts, we must not suppose that by combining them we would have a **complete** list of all the gifts that God gives and that are available to His people. To do so would be presumptuous on our part and put a fairly small box around the possibilities that God may choose to employ. Let us rather consider the specifics of these "lists" as guidelines for how God gifts His people, in a diversified unity, for the purpose of serving Him. In so doing, we leave God to do His work in the inner man as He desires even if it does not fit into our neat, little compartments.

We must note right away that the reason these gifts are commonly referred to as *"spiritual gifts"* is that they are specially empowered by the Spirit of God Himself. We see this implied in Romans 12, but it is directly spelled out when Paul states, *"But one and the same Spirit works all these things, distributing to each one individually just as He wills"* (1 Corinthians 12:11). It may help some readers to think of the phrase *"gifts of the Spirit"* to help retain this clarification.

This distinguishes these "gifts" from other natural abilities and talents. There are, for example, gifted authors who are able to communicate exceptionally well to their readers about a variety of subjects. Many of these, obviously, do not have a personal relationship with Christ and therefore do not have the Spirit of Christ residing within them. As a result, they have not been given a *"gift of the Spirit."* There may be great talent and ability, and that talent and ability is no doubt a gift of God as a representation of Himself within man who was created in His image, but this is wholly different than the spiritual gifting received as a result of a relationship with Christ.

The same can be said of the musician, or the teacher, or the public speaker, or the mechanic, or the baseball player. All have great talents and abilities, but unless there is the indwelling of the Spirit of God there are no *"gifts of the Spirit"* present in their lives. It is important to keep this in mind, for if one of these were to respond to Christ in faith, the spiritual gift(s) they receive may, or may not, coincide with the natural abilities they possess. Let us not mistake talent for giftedness and raise people to levels of responsibility within the Body of Christ for which they are not spiritually ready or sufficiently gifted by God to serve in a specific capacity.

It is a very telling sign in our local churches when persons are placed in positions of leadership and influence because of apparent success in their jobs, their finances, in some political arena, or as a performer rather than in response to their spiritual walk and spiritual gifts. The Biblical pattern, and criteria, for leadership in the Body of Christ is clear and defined in these passages, and filled out completely in other passages. We must be diligent to follow these guidelines, especially when they may not make complete sense to us. Success in business and other endeavors does not necessarily translate to success as a spiritual leader.

Before moving forward, let me quote the main verses from First Corinthians 12. It would benefit the reader, as well, to read through each of the four passages mentioned above to gain an overall context. I will quote and reference verses, as I comment, from each of these passages as evidence for the conclusions being drawn. In First Corinthians 12 we find these words:

Now there are varieties of gifts, but the same Spirit.
And there are varieties of ministries, and the same

Lord. And there are varieties of effects, but the same God who works all things in all persons. But to each one is given the manifestation of the Spirit for the common good. (1 Corinthians 12:4-7)

But one and the same Spirit works all these things, distributing to each one individually just as He wills. For even as the body is one and yet has many members, and all the members of the body, though they are many, are as one body, so also is Christ. (1 Corinthians 12:11-12)

If the foot should say, "Because I am not a hand, I am not a part of the body," it is not for this reason any the less a part of the body. And if the ear should say, "Because I am not an eye, I am not a part of the body," it is not for this reason any the less a part of the body. If the whole body were an eye, where would the hearing be? If the whole were hearing, where would the sense of smell be? But now God has placed the members, each one of them, in the body, just as He desired. (1 Corinthians 12:15-18)

A main characteristic of spiritual gifts found in these words is that they are **God-given**. This may seem an obvious point, but we must thoroughly understand how directly God is involved in the gifting of His people. Not only is He involved with the gifting; he is thoroughly and completely involved in His totality. See how each person of the Trinity is involved in the giving. Note that verses 4-7 reference the "*Spirit,*" the "*Lord*" (by which is meant Christ), as well as "*God*" (by which is meant the Father). God's participation in giving gifts to each individual is a foundation stone to developing the proper working of the church (i.e., the Body of Christ) as a whole. This is God in His Trinity moving among His people to bring glory to Himself.

God actively places each person in the proper "spot" in the body so that the body will function correctly (1 Corinthians 12:11, 18). If a person is out of place, the church can only act as a crippled body. Paul uses very clear language in this regard in Ephesians 4:16 by stating that the church, as His body, must be *"fitted and held together by that which every joint supplies, according to the proper working of each individual part."* The analogy of the body is appropriate here, and quite fitting. Have you ever noticed that a pain, or some damage, in one part of your body affects the entire body? Even a broken toe, as small a part as it is, dramatically alters our ability to live life in a normal way—the way we are supposed to live—walking, moving, running, playing. The Body of Christ is exactly this way, except the "broken toes" are people with hurts and pain, people with sin and denial. These believers are people God has gifted to serve as part of a greater whole, but they are afflicted and crippled. This does not just affect them it affects us all. The use of gifts in serving one another is to be healing for the individual being served, but then lead to a "healed" community as well. A community that is a healthy, vibrant, effective Body of Christ.

Another main characteristic we find is the unequivocal purpose for the spiritual gifts God has placed in our lives: to serve one another (1 Corinthians 12:7). This service to others is our service to God. Peter says it as plainly as possible: *"As each one* (of us who are Christians) *has received a special gift, employ it in serving one another, as good stewards of the manifold grace of God"* (1 Peter 4:10). God has crafted the Body of Christ in such a way that as we serve others, we will also be served, and together we can serve those around us. When there is a gap in the body—a hurting person, one distracted by sin, or one unwilling to share his or her gift—someone else suffers. There may not be another person who can fill the need, and so the need goes unmet, because the body is broken.

A broken body is one in which growth is stunted, and this is absolutely true in the church which is His Body as well. The words in Ephesians show the results of a body functioning properly, with all of its parts healthy and engaged. Paul reveals that it *"causes the growth of the body for the building up of itself in love"* (Ephesians 4:16) and that we are to *"grow up in all aspects into Him, who is the head, even Christ"* (Ephesians 4:15). Just like our physical body, the Body of Christ grows and becomes stronger as each part functions as created by God.

This leads to the essential element of unity within the body. But it is a unity that is completely filled with diversity. Note that Paul uses the phrases *"varieties of gifts...varieties of ministries...varieties of effects"* (1 Corinthians 12:4-7) and then conditions this aspect of variety, or diversity, with the concept of the *"common good"* (1 Corinthians 12:7). The passage in Romans 12:4-5 puts it this way: *"For just as we have many members in one body and all the members do not have the same function, so we, who are many, are one body in Christ, and individually members one of another."* Someone once said, "Variety is the spice of life," and God certainly intends for His church to be flavored with spices of all kinds.

This concept of God's gifts to us as individuals, for the purpose of serving the community as a whole, should help put an end to envy and strife within the ranks of congregations. This idea can really be empowering and give great security when each person is taught, and learns, that they are important and necessary parts of the Body of Christ. Yet, even pastors are at times threatened by those around them with differing gifts and abilities. Instead of working together, our selfish nature causes us to undermine the contributions of others in order to retain what we think is our rightful place among those around us. Unfortunately, insecurity on the part of pastors and leaders is the cause of much suppression of the giftedness of God's people. Rather, we should rejoice and support those around us who fill those gaps that our own giftedness cannot fill. This type of unselfishness and support for others does not seem that difficult, but it is.

The variety, or diversity, of the gifts God bestows is actually a representation of His character. Peter calls it the *"manifold grace of God"* (1 Peter 4:10). The word manifold inherently speaks to the idea of variety. God's grace comes to us in a variety of ways—the love of a mother to a child, the sweetness of the spring air, the incarnation of His Son—and He seeks to show that variety in the many, many ways He gifts His people.

God's purpose for the church is a continuation of the purpose for which Christ came into the world, and that purpose is continued redemption (see Ephesians 1:22-23 and Colossians 1:24-27). This is an element of the concept of the Body of **Christ** that is often overlooked. His body—the redeemed people of God, the Church—functions on behalf of Christ in the world. He is the head of this body (Colossians 1:18) and leads and directs its activity. We are the members, the parts, of the body that move and act according to His desires. As was already pointed out, He gives gifts according to His will and desire. Our obedience (remember the response of faith in worship like Abraham) is the truest measure of our life of worship.

Discovering your Gifts

That a person might have to "discover" his or her gifts may seem a strange notion. It is evident, at whatever age we may come to Christ as Savior, that changes begin to take place that otherwise may have never happened, and depending on the solidity of former habits and patterns, we must learn and grow. This is the concept that theologians refer to as sanctification; that is, the daily growing and maturing in our faith that begins the moment we receive Christ.

The discovery and development of the gifts God gives through the Spirit are part of this process. Remember that though God expects and desires to use our talents and abilities once they are redeemed, this does not necessarily spell out the area of our spiritual gifts. If variety is a key characteristic of spiritual gifts, we can even expect it in the microcosm of our own lives. Our God-given gifts may complement our natural abilities, and God certainly expects us to commit these to Him as well. What I am describing is a process of discovery and a commitment to serve with what He has given us.

The simplest way to begin a "search" for our gifts is through a "Spiritual Gifts Assessment" or questionnaire. These take several forms, the most common being a list of many questions for which you score your own tendencies in various areas. By adding up your "scores" you find the three or four gifts that you seem to show, usually from the compiled list of gifts out of the four main New Testament passages. I have included a reference for one of these types of questionnaires in Appendix A. These are useful, but limited in their scope, and I would strongly suggest that the use of one of these questionnaires must also be combined with one or more of the following methods of discovery.

A second method, and quite important, is to spend time reading and re-reading the main passages on gifts found in the Bible. Pray through these passages, asking God to help you understand the overall concept of spiritual gifts, as well as reveal how He has gifted you to serve those around you. You might have a notebook handy to jot down thoughts that come to mind, questions to seek answers for, or examples of how various gifts seem to be evident in your life. Your own observations in these matters are a positive stepping-stone in your journey.

Be careful, however, that you avoid looking for evidence in your own life of the gifts that appear "important" to you, or are important according to some kind of worldly standard. For example, if you think that being a teacher (or pastor, or administrator, or whatever) is an important role in the church, and you decide that you must have that gift because God would obviously trust you with such a vital gift...then watch out! Pride is coming through the door, and you may be missing the real blessing that God is giving you with your true gifts. With each gift comes responsibility, and the ones that seem more important may carry a level of responsibility for which you are not prepared. God places you exactly where He wants you, and then He has given you the gifts and grace to fulfill your mission. Once you find it, and serve Him this way, you will be completely satisfied with your role because each role is significant and important. God has made them so. Keep this in mind, and explore all of these avenues for discovering your gifts so you can serve Him with all that you are.

Another important way to discover your spiritual gifts is to get in the game and serve! God cannot direct you and guide you in service if you are not serving, just like you cannot steer a car if it is not moving. A parked car does not change course no matter how much you turn the wheel. In the same way, if you jump in and begin to serve in children's ministry and come to find out that it does not fit your gifts very well, then God can begin to steer you into another path as you listen to the needs of people and seek to serve them. But please, please, please do not back out of any commitments you have already made to a ministry (if you offered to teach First Grade girls for a quarter, then complete your commitment). This experience will help you grow in your Christian walk, and the need for integrity in fulfilling any commitment you made is great.

The observations of trusted and mature Christians who know you and observe how you live your life is another way to help discover your gifts. Mature believers will be familiar with the concept of spiritual gifts and will have seen many positive examples of gifts helping to build the Body of Christ. Mature believers will have taken (and continue to take) the journey in discovering and developing their own gifts, and will be more than willing to help others do the same. Ask questions like: How do you see me effectively serving God's people? Are there strengths and weaknesses in the way that I interact with others? What would you say are the two or three spiritual gifts that are evident in my life? Do you see potential in my life in an area that I am not currently using?

This external observation can be compared with any questionnaire you might have used, as well as your own personal study, prayer, and observations. As you compare notes from all of these sources, a clearer picture of your God-given spiritual gifts will come out. You will begin to see the unique blend of gifts that God has given, and your excitement at using them and developing them will grow. As your internal momentum builds, and God refines your understanding of spiritual gifts and their place in the church, your responsibility for developing and using those gifts increases as well.

Developing Spiritual Gifts

Although the gifts we receive at salvation are from God, we must immediately begin to share in the responsibility to develop them and use them in our life of worship. Scripture is clear that the Christian life is a mutual working relationship between God and the believer. Paul writes, *"Work out your own salvation with fear and trembling, for it is God who is at work in you to will and to work for His good pleasure"* (Philippians 2:12-13).

In reference to this idea of God's work and our work, there are those who argue that God is so much in control that we are puppets (He is absolutely sovereign), and there are others who say that we have the ability to choose and direct our lives as we see fit (total "free" will). While there appears to be a direct conflict, for one cannot apparently be a "puppet" and also make their own "choices," it is nonetheless the case that both are true. This is what it means for Paul to say, *"work out your salvation"* and *"for it is God who is at work in you"* in the same sentence in Philippians.

We must not fall into the trap of trying to reconcile these two realities based upon our own experience. On our level of being, or existence, having someone else in control and us being in control are contradictory. However, God's nature is such that He exists differently than humanity. His level of being, or existence, is something altogether unlike what we are. Only by allowing for this distinction can we come to understand, in a limited way, that He can be totally and completely sovereign (and Scripture teaches that He is); and that we can be completely responsible for our lives and actions (which Scripture also teaches).

And so, we hold a certain responsibility for developing and exercising our gifts as God intended. As I already mentioned, God has given these gifts for the benefit of others and the members of the Christian church specifically. To selfishly ignore this overarching purpose of His grace to us would be to sin against His Spirit that indwells us with these gifts. We are not to use these gifts for our own personal gain. This does not mean that it is sinful to make a living in the service of God, but it does mean that taking advantage of people because you are "gifted" in order to further your own career is not favorable in God's eyes.

Let me offer some specifics as to how gifts, once a person becomes aware of them, can be developed and enhanced for greater effectiveness. And it is effectiveness that we are after. God expects the Body of Christ, and each part of it, to work properly (Ephesians 4:15-16). In order for this to happen each part must understand their unique contribution and how to do it in such a way that it enhances the ministry and growth of the whole body.

There are at least five general principles, maybe more, to help us develop our gifts. Incidentally, these five principles can be used in many other areas of life as well, such as with our personality types, natural talents and abilities, relationships, etc. The items are not listed in any strict order. I have known many people who actively serve the Body of Christ with their gifts but could not necessarily identify their "gift" from a list. They simply love God, love people, and meet the needs that they are able to meet. Life is too unpredictable to say that it has to happen "this way" or that you can do it best "that way," so allow some flexibility in your own journey as well.

First, we must have an **awareness** of our gifts. This we already dealt with extensively above in the section titled "Discovering Your Gifts."

Second, we must seek further **understanding**, or comprehension, of how our gifts "fit" in the overall scheme of things. We should be aware of how our gifts interact with the gifts of others around us. We can identify others with complementary gifts and serve alongside them. Think of yourself, using another analogy, as a piece of a jigsaw puzzle. Somewhere in the midst of these 1000 pieces, you fit—*and only you fit in that spot*! In order for the full picture to come together, you must fit together with the pieces around you, who in turn, fit with other pieces. Ultimately, when every piece of the puzzle is in place, a beautiful picture appears. And it is only complete when every piece is there.

It is a great feeling when that last piece is put in place and you can see the complete puzzle.

Third, we must **study God's word**. In this context you might think that I am simply suggesting a study of the various passages on spiritual gifts. This, for certain, would be very helpful but it would also be shortsighted. God's word must penetrate our lives daily and regularly from the beginning of Genesis to the end of Revelation. We can only know the true nature of spiritual gifts when we know about the nature of the church as Christ's body. We can only know these things by knowing Christ. We must also know the uniqueness of the church in the history of redemption. We must see a bigger and broader picture that can only come by daily reading and study.

Fourth, our gifts require us **to serve**. Not only can we discover our gifts by serving, but also when we serve our gifts become refined. God prepares us today for what He needs us for in the future. He gave us gifts to serve, and as we serve He will work in us to grow us for His glory and pleasure. I cannot say it enough (or rather, repeat what Scripture says enough): **serving others is the reason God gives you and I gifts.**

Fifth, we can develop by **observing** others with similar gifts. Look around, and when you see someone serving in an area that seems to fit with your gifts and interest, introduce yourself. Ask to help. Learn and be taught. The Church is a body of people that has been around a long, long time and you are not a lone ranger. We are part of a team. Work with your teammates and get moving!

I have been brief in this area of development because much of it will overlap with my discussion on the life of worship as a life of love and service that will challenge and encourage you in your daily walk with Christ.

Refining and Focusing your Gifts

I have mentioned that we should not confuse our natural abilities and talents with our spiritual gifts, and it is important to keep that distinction in mind. We do, however, want to recognize the **value** of our natural talents, and how they relate to and interact with our spiritual gifts. That a person may have a talent for public speaking and then be gifted by God with the gifts of wisdom and teaching will mean a powerful, divinely appointed message coming to those who hear. This is an instance in which a **talent** and a **gift** work in tandem for greater effectiveness.

This is not surprising in that God is the God who redeems us entirely and completely—as a whole person. It is not only our soul that interests Him, but also our spirit, our body, our personality, our passions, our talents, our emotions and all that represents who we are. His hand touches every part of our lives and the redemption found in Christ is meant to transform every area of our lives. With this in mind, we can understand how He might refine and focus our gifts as they interact with the different aspects of ministry and others who serve alongside us.

Let us look at our personalities as well. It is obvious when there are two or more people together that different people are...well...different. We respond in a myriad of ways to the same stimulus. When we see a beautiful sunset some of us sigh, some of us grunt, some of us run for a camera to save the memory, some of us analyze the light waves as they enter the atmosphere, producing the various effects of color across the horizon due to the interaction of the light with dust particles floating throughout the terrestrial atmosphere...you get the idea. These responses are based on that internal part of us commonly known as "personality."

Personalities, of course, are neither good nor bad. They just are. They are all distorted by sin, so in that sense they are not what they were meant to be, but in any case that at least puts us all on the same playing field. So, let us for now say that personality is neutral. No one has the market cornered on having the "right" kind of personality. This being true, then each response to the sunset is in itself an honest response. None are right or wrong, but simply responses to the stimulus of the sunset, based upon the internal characteristics of the responder.

I point this out to help us realize the diversity of personalities in the human race. There are several "personality profile" instruments that exist to help individuals understand their own personality "type." My own favorite is called the *Meyers-Briggs Temperament Indicator* (MBTI). The MBTI shows a series of sixteen personality "types." However, rather than each one representing one-sixteenth of the population, it allows for a huge variety within each type. Essentially, the MBTI explains categories that are identifiable enough for us to find which of the sixteen types we identify with, but allows room within that type for us to be completely unique as individuals. In this way it represents the reality of our daily lives and helps us to understand ourselves, and others, better.

When brought alongside the concept of spiritual gifts, discovering and understanding our personality type can also enhance our service for the Lord. We can identify strengths and weaknesses that might help or hinder the ministry that God desires for us. We can see that when the person with a gentle, accepting personality type is combined with the spiritual gifts of helps and mercy that he or she can excel at caring for and walking alongside those who are hurting and in need. Again, God redeems the whole person and wants these different aspects of life to work together.

Another area that is important to define and refine our gifts is our own interests and desires. Some refer to this as

passion. What excites you, keeps you up at night talking, and to which you will devote time, energy, and money without any expectation of return? To what cause does your heart "leap" when it is discussed? If you were able to attend your own funeral, what would you like to hear being said about you? What kind of people do you like to be with, spend time with? These types of questions help to focus and guide your gifts and will help you to discover your passion. Passion helps us to know where to use our gifts.

For example, if a believer has an interest in children and his heart is moved every time he hears a report about the need for Sunday School teachers, then he should respond by helping in that ministry area. As he serves a term teaching Fifth Grade boys, he might find that his passion is being further clarified as he hears the stories of boys without fathers in the home. His heart goes out to them, and ***after*** he finishes his commitment in the Sunday School program, he moves over to the Big Brother/Big Sister program that the church sponsors. Interestingly, as he serves there and spends time with several boys, the need for a coordinator comes along within the ministry and his ***spiritual gift*** of administration, along with his love and desire to work with kids, as well as his previous experience of organizing (using his spiritual gift) and teaching a Sunday School class, makes him the ideal choice for the position. Ultimately, he serves in this capacity for many years.

This is how the journey of discovering and developing spiritual gifts happens. God is at work in you as you are at work serving Him by serving others. When our God-given spiritual giftedness becomes discovered and developed, we become useful tools for God's purposes. While you walk along this path you will find renewed energy and stamina to serve when you are truly living a life of worship. A life in which you are doing what God created you to do for His glory.

A Life of Love and Service

Combining all of these aspects to create a life of worship may seem to be a daunting task. Allowing God to transform us by renewing our minds, and then discovering and using our spiritual gifts, takes time. Do not assume that all of this will happen overnight, or in the next year, or in the next decade. Our life as Christians is one of growth and maturing. As we move forward we become more comfortable with the process that is inherent in learning the ways of God, and to listening and obeying the Spirit residing within us.

It should be a comfort to us that God is not solely relying on our own ability to produce the kind of life that would honor Him day after day. He is moving in us and around us, behind us and before us. He is our great Partner and Companion, the Leader and Sustainer, the Prompter and Provider. We can do nothing without Him, yet everything through Him that He might desire us to do (Philippians 4:13). He is always there to love us, care for us, and nurture us in our faith and to help this process of growth.

With these things in mind, let us look at the end result of all that we have discussed thus far. Our consideration in Part II of this book has already covered spiritual gifts and their development. We have looked into the importance of "renewing the mind" and allowing a transformation to take place that moves from our internal thought life into the external realm of action. Finally, let us examine the **activity** of worship in life, what I would like to call: *a life of love and service*.

God's Hand

We must once again be reminded that the reality of salvation is God's work through Christ, given to us as a free gift. The Holy Spirit comes to reside within us at the moment of salvation and brings spiritual gifts for us to serve God and His people, the Body of Christ. As we learn and grow in our daily Christian walk, God works in us and through us to set us apart (sanctify us) for Himself. He is in our lives from the moment we respond to Him in faith and continuously from then on.

Ephesians 2:8-10 is one of the purest and most succinct descriptions of the life of the believer from salvation all the way through sanctification (the process of learning to live the Christian life). It is unfortunate that so many believers have heard and understand verses eight and nine, but never seem to have noticed the significance of verse ten. Here we will look at the three verses as completely and vitally interconnected:

> *For by grace you have been saved through faith, and that not of yourselves, it is the gift of God; not as a result of works, that no one should boast. For we are His workmanship, created in Christ Jesus for good works, which God prepared beforehand, that we should walk in them.* (Ephesians 2:8-10)

Verses eight and nine clearly remind us that our works count for nothing in regards to earning or deserving a restored relationship with God. Salvation is a gift and the faith that we have to respond to His call is a gift. This allows for no pride or deservedness on our part. We do not deserve what we have received, and that fact alone should cause us to overflow with gratitude and love for God. Beyond this free gift of salvation and faith, He has blessed us with every spiritual blessing, as explained by Paul earlier in Ephesians 1:3-14. Truly our response to God for His love and His gifts should be one of love and obedience.

And that leads to verse ten. God not only gives us salvation, but He then molds us and shapes us to be more than we ever imagined. The idea behind the phrase, *"We are His workmanship,"* is that God is creating a great masterpiece. The wording suggests the imagery of a master artist with his most incredible, creative piece of art. God's hand is at work in us, on us, for us, to make us magnificent pieces of His own creative endeavors.

And for what? Why is He creatively working within us? *For good works*! Do not miss the connection between good works and the concept of worship. God's goal for us is to serve Him and worship Him in the pursuit of good works that He prepares for us. Before we even know it is there, an opportunity to serve others is placed in our life by God, that we may serve Him by serving them. This is the truest life of worship. This is serving God.

Colossians 1:9-10 has a very similar statement. A prayer is written for believers,

> *...that you may be filled with the knowledge of His will in all spiritual wisdom and understanding, so that you may walk in a manner worthy of the Lord, to please Him in all respects, bearing fruit in every good work and increasing in the knowledge of God.*

Note the repeated pattern of internal knowledge and wisdom *("filled with the knowledge of His will")* expressing itself externally in a walk of good works *("bearing fruit in every good work")*. As I write and study in preparing this manuscript, these Scriptures continue to cry out that worship is to be seen as holistic and life-encompassing. For us to relegate the discussion of worship primarily to a

Sunday morning event has been to short circuit the reality of worship in our lives. Is it really any wonder that there appears to be such a great chasm between the "beliefs" and the daily lives of so many Christians?

Note the phrase *"that you may walk in a manner worthy of the Lord, to please Him in all respects."* Rather than misrepresent Jesus' words in John 4:23-24 about worshiping in spirit and truth, claiming that there is a right way to worship and a wrong way to worship, as many have done (see complete comments in Chapter 5), it would benefit us to recognize that *all* believers worship in their daily walk. However, their worship may not always be in a worthy manner or be pleasing God in all respects. This is true because the evidence of a true heart of worship is not based upon the right feeling about God, or the right music, or anything of that nature. The evidence is *"bearing fruit in every good work."* Otherwise there is such a disconnect between the idea of worship and our daily lives that we could rightfully wonder how the two could ever relate.

This is the essence of why it is so important for us to *think* about worship in the right way. Worship as a concept is so much broader than normally presented that we must begin to re-think and re-form our teaching on the subject.

The Imitation of Christ

Another aspect of a life of worship exemplified in a life of love and service is that of imitating Christ. Scripture certainly teaches that Christ is to be our example. We read such statements as, *"For you have been called for this purpose, since Christ also suffered for you, leaving you an example for you to follow in His steps"* (1 Peter 2:21), and that we are to be *"conformed to the image of His Son"* (Romans 8:29). There is a difference here between following

Christ's example and trying to copy His lifestyle. Let me explain.

Obedience is the central ingredient of Christ's example, and the point at which we are to follow Him closely. What many people fail to recognize is that we are not necessarily following His example when we copy something that He did during His lifetime. Celibacy, for instance, was part of His life on earth, yet He does not expect all believers to copy this aspect of His life. In fact, celibacy is actually a special "gifting" that is for some believers (see 1 Corinthians 7), rather than an expectation for all. Some have misapplied this to mean that men and women are somehow more "holy" if unmarried than married, yet this is surely not the case. It becomes a matter of copying rather than following an example of obedience.

Christians have focused on other areas of Christ's life with the assumption that copying Jesus' lifestyle somehow makes them more holy or acceptable before God, as though the lifestyle was the substance of His righteousness. As we have seen, someone's lifestyle is a reflection of his or her internal belief system. Christ lived the way that He did, and did the things He did, out of obedience to the Father. This is why obedience, unwavering and total obedience, is the example that Christ has given us to follow.

Christ's **path** of obedience was teaching, suffering, dying and resurrecting to ultimately re-claim His position at God's right hand. If copying these actions of His life were truly God's intention, then we are all quite behind in the race. It is, rather, **His obedience and submission to God's will** that is our example. Peter writes, *"For you have been called for this purpose, since Christ also suffered for you, leaving an example for you to follow in His steps"* (1 Peter 2:21). Although there is some element of common suffering that we will experience, it is more directly Christ's obedience to the Father and His trust in God's faithfulness that Peter is holding out to us as an example. Rather than copy His works, we should emulate His faith and be obedient in our own circumstances.

When we speak of a life of love and service we must realize that God is designing for us a path to follow. He is calling us to, and gifting us for, a path that is uniquely ours. This is a path He has prepared for us. It has not been created for anyone else. We are to be obedient to His calling by using our gifts and walking in the good works He prepares. This is our path, and this is the life that reflects the example of obedience given to us. And, by the way, our path intersects and intertwines with the paths of others in the Body of Christ so that we as a community follow the path God has given our church. It is beautiful, and truly a masterpiece, if you dwell on it.

In the last decade there has been a campaign to apparently help Christians, especially youth, think about the actions they take and reactions that they have on a daily basis. The campaign, or movement, used an acronym with the letters WWJD. These four letters stand for "What Would Jesus Do?" Bracelets, shoestrings, T-shirts, Bible covers, and every other imaginable piece of saleable merchandise were printed with "WWJD." The idea was to ask the question, "What would Jesus do?" and respond to life and circumstances based upon the answer to the question.

Although the whole WWJD movement may have raised a certain awareness level in the minds of Christians to be aware of our reactions to life situations, I am not so sure that the question was the right one to be asking. The way that *Jesus* may, or may not, have reacted in any situation is not necessarily the way that *we* should respond. If God had wanted Jesus to be here and respond, He would have been here. What He did do was put *us* here to respond, and our obedient response is what we must figure out and the one we are responsible for.

It seems that this movement was a reduction of the message of Charles Sheldon's great work, *In His Steps*.[46] In his narrative Sheldon relays the stories of individuals as they wrestle through the real-life process of living life in the steps of Christ. One of the questions they ask is, "What would Jesus do?" The substance behind this question, however, is deeper than the copying of Jesus' lifestyle in the way that they live. Their decisions were motivated by internal spiritual growth that was demonstrated in their daily lives.

It would give us better perspective if we were to rather ask ourselves the question, "How would God have *me* respond in this situation or to this person?" Granted, we can look at Christ's responses and activities in the New Testament and sometimes draw parallels with our own situation, however we have to admit that more often than not we are in uncharted territory and God has still asked us to respond, reply and react. This is why this discussion on the life of worship has been so extensive and full-orbed. We need an underlying framework, a foundation, to respond to life in such a way that will coincide with Biblical principles and a Christian worldview. That is what renewing the mind is all about, that is why God has given us gifts, and that is why we must learn to *think* about life so that we can *act* out a life of love and service.

Loving and Serving

I have said before that the way we live a life of worship is to serve God by serving others, and we serve others best when we love them. The passages on love are so numerous that I am not sure which ones to comment on or which ones might give the best summary of the love God wants His people to show one another.

Love operates, even in the Body of Christ, on all kinds of different levels. We cannot expect to "feel" the same love toward a mere acquaintance that we do toward our family member or a close friend. At times, even family members and friends require different levels of love, and we might not even "feel" loving toward them at all.

Beginning in Philippians 2:1-5 would be appropriate in this discussion, since we find here another concrete way in which Christ is to be our example:

> *If there is any encouragement in Christ, if there is any consolation of love, if there is any fellowship of the Spirit, if any affection and compassion, make my joy complete by being of the same mind, maintaining the same love, united in spirit, intent on one purpose.*
>
> *Do nothing from selfishness or empty conceit, but with humility of mind let each of you regard one another as more important than himself, do not merely look out for your own interests, but also for the interest of others. Have this attitude in yourselves which was also in Christ Jesus.*

Paul places these verses in the context of love, in general, in the first two verses and then gets very specific as to what that means in real life—and more importantly in our attitudes, for our attitudes will direct our actions.

Notice the activities associated with these ideas of maintaining love, having unity and commitments to the same goals and purpose. "*Affection*" and "*compassion*" are specific, tangible actions we can take that do not necessarily require us to "feel" love in any way. We can show affection and compassion because it is the right thing to do, and that in and of itself is love. Paul also mentions "*consolation*" and "*fellowship.*" Again, neither of these requires any special "feeling" of love; these ideas represent the actions that love can take.

What is evident is that love can be acted upon regardless of the feeling associated with the object of the loving act. Consider Christ, as Paul describes Him later in Philippians 2:6-8,

> *Who, although He existed in the form of God, did not regard equality with God a thing to be grasped, but emptied Himself, taking the form of a bond-servant, being made in the likeness of men. And being found in appearance as a man, He humbled Himself to the point of death, even death on a cross.*

Christ showed love by being made "*in the likeness of men*" and if that was not low enough (He was God, after all), He was obedient to the point of death on a cross. I am not sure that Christ had a "feeling" of love toward the world at the point of His death, yet we describe His sacrifice as the ultimate demonstration of love. We are called to act out love in the same manner, even when we do not feel like it.

It is this demonstration of love that is to be our attitude, just like that attitude of Christ. We are to look out for the interests of others—period. We are to regard them as more important than ourselves—period. This describes love, and the **attitude** that love takes, which will ultimately determine the **action** that love takes. Hmmm...this sounds really familiar, as though we have covered it before—***the internal thought is expressed in the external action***.

Love is active. And it is active regardless of the feeling associated with it. Why is this distinction important? Because we are human and we hurt each other. In spite of our best efforts to treat each other with dignity and honor, we slip up, say or do something that would have been better left unsaid or undone, and someone gets hurt. You have been hurt. I have been hurt. And to top it off, we have been hurt by other Christians, our brothers and sisters in Christ. We are told to love them, but they have hurt us—now what?

The beauty of this type of love, that Jesus demonstrates and we are to emulate, is that we can show love in actions that communicate caring, compassion, consolation, fellowship, dignity, protection, and on and on. When we actively love, we are active.

Of course, we do feel better when what is happening inside of us (how we are "feeling") is congruent with what we are doing on the outside. This is not always possible, and that is why I suggest recognizing the levels of love in all the relationships around us. Our feelings are shifty, and are at times not to be trusted, so we may have to act the way God's word teaches us in spite of our own feelings. (Maybe this is part of what Jesus meant when He said we must "*deny ourselves.*")

The closer the relationship (husband, wife, children, parents), the more we "feel" the love inside that we are demonstrating on the outside. Otherwise it would be a bleak existence. On the other hand, are we to stop demonstrating love toward those who are close to us when we do not "feel" love on the inside? No, of course not. Love is active regardless of the feelings that we may be having at the time.

In a similar way, we must demonstrate love to those who may have hurt us in one way or another. The "love chapter" of the Bible (1 Corinthians 13) teaches us many more practical and tangible ways to demonstrate love at every level of relationship. Does someone irritate you? Be patient and kind. Did someone get recognition that you thought you deserved? Do not be jealous or brag, or seek your own due. Were you hurt or maligned, justly or unjustly? Avoid holding a grudge and keeping score. Believe the truth you find around you, hope for the best in all your circumstances, and endure these earthly trials with patience. Seek to build people up, rather than tear them down. These are the activities of love.

Is this easy? No, but it can get easier. Or maybe it will not get easier, but it can become more habitual. Love is a matter of practice, after all. Yes, you read that correctly. *We must practice the activities of love.* In a culture that provides most everything in a moment, or faster, there is still the matter of love that we must practice daily and learn to live daily. Many, many things change instantaneously when we come to Christ in faith, and yet the many activities of daily life we must learn by practicing. One of those practices is love.

The Life of Love and Service

And so we must practice and grow in our daily Christian walk. We must practice a life of worship. We must practice love, the use of our gifts, renewing the mind, discerning the pitfalls of our culture and the world around us. We practice making decisions every day based on what God is teaching us in His word. As we learn and grow we will love God and serve Him by loving others and serving them. We will worship by living a life of love and service.

Balance

Throughout this discussion I hope that the reader will hear the emphasis that is placed on the concept of balance. Balancing the internal and the external. Balancing thought with action. Balancing the whole of worship as a lifestyle that transcends all aspects of personal and corporate life. And later, balancing the four aspects of corporate worship, or balancing the various elements of corporate worship. We must continually assess the balance found in our personal lives, our family lives, and the life of the Body of Christ.

I would like to spend some time addressing a specific area of balance that really is the crux of what I have been saying. There are some who may be thinking that I have been undermining the concept of the corporate gathering of worship because I have de-emphasized it in order to promote the idea of worship as a lifestyle. In fact, I *have* emphasized the lifestyle aspect because biblically it is a much broader concept into which corporate worship fits.

We can find in Scripture that there is a balance that must be maintained between words (or beliefs) and service (or actions). I think we can safely expand this to be a balance between: a) what most people believe worship to be as the opportunity to address God in praise, and; b) what I have sought to present as the broader concept of worship as a lifestyle of love and service. We find this balance in a number of New Testament passages,[47] but let us look at one in particular that gives a clear picture of what this balance looks like.

Hebrews 13:15-16 states:

*Through Him then, let us continually offer up a
sacrifice of praise to God, that is, the fruit of lips that
give thanks to His name. And do not neglect doing
good and sharing; for with such sacrifices God is
pleased.*

Stopping Short

Many of us are familiar with verse fifteen of this passage,
*"Through Him then, let us continually offer up a sacrifice of
praise to God, that is, the fruit of lips that give thanks to His
name."* There are several praise choruses or worship songs
that adapt this verse. Others contain similar phrases and
these words have become memorable because a melody has
been attached.

Of course, this verse offers excellent counsel not only for
our personal praises, but also for the praises of the gathered
community. Note the reminder by the author of Hebrews
that our access to God is through Christ. The whole concept
of access to God is a sub-theme within the book of Hebrews,
and actually a very interesting study on its own. At this
point in Hebrews the author reminds the reader that the
proper method of approaching God is through Christ, and
thus when coming to praise God the Father the name of
Christ must be on our lips.

I think the idea brought forth by the word "continually" is
important here, and underscores the fact that our praise
cannot just be during a designated time of "worship." Our
praise and thanksgiving must come to God on a daily, hourly
and continual basis. The praise of our lips is a sacrifice: a
spiritual sacrifice of a daily walk of worship. When you carry
this concept to its logical conclusion you discover that there
must be something more to worship than singing some
songs and saying some prayers. Otherwise, our pursuit of

"continually" praising God would lead to some kind of monastic lifestyle totally separated from the realities of life.

The author of Hebrews has in mind the contrast between the spiritual sacrifice that Christians make and the physical animal sacrifices of the Jews. "The author uses [the word sacrifice] of the only sacrifices Christians offer, spiritual sacrifices. So he urges them to offer...a sacrifice consisting of praise. The thought that the sacrifice Christians offer is spiritual occurs elsewhere, as in Romans 12:1."[48]

When we consider the sacrifice of praise in relation to our corporate worship, we think of joyous, thankful songs that help us to remember what God has done for us, in us, and in the midst of our lives. We might also think of the sacrifice of praise in our daily lives, and as the above quote suggests, draw this verse in Hebrews close together with Romans 12. Spiritual sacrifices are both verbal and the presentation of our bodies. As I have said, this is a response to God and appropriate recognition of His activity on behalf of His people. Sometimes the praise becomes contagious and even hearts that are downcast are brought up in thanksgiving to God.

But why is it considered a "*sacrifice?*" Maybe the best explanation is that when we offer praise to God, we are forced to stop thinking about ourselves and admonished to focus on God. That we are told to do this continually becomes a real sacrifice—a sacrifice of our pride and selfishness. Have you ever really tried to think about God's work among His people, only to have your thoughts turn to your own situation and problems after only a matter of minutes? It is hard work to focus away from yourself. I wonder if we really considered this aspect of sacrifice, if the praise we offer to God really is sacrificial?

And so we are together for "worship" within the church walls, we praise, we offer thanks and we worship. Time to go home now. Why do we stop short at verse fifteen and overlook the unity of thought as it flows to verse sixteen? The songs and choruses I mentioned earlier do not seem to continue the flow of thought found in Scripture into the next verse. The presentation and teaching on worship does not move beyond verse fifteen in order to consider sixteen. Why not?

The Other Sacrifices

My slightly sarcastic comment in the previous paragraph, "Time to go home now," is really part of my overall point in bringing out the balance in these verses of Hebrews. Once we spend time together as a corporate body praising and thanking God for all His goodness in our lives, we have to go home. ***Ultimately, the praise and thanksgiving—the sacrifices, if they are to continue—must continue at home***.

And this is what verse sixteen is all about, *"And do not neglect doing good and sharing; for with such sacrifices God is pleased."* The author of Hebrews seems to know in advance that some Christians will come to church and do their "praise and worship," then head home and neglect the rest of their responsibility as Christians. He warns, *"Do not neglect doing good and sharing."* This is interesting, for he anticipates the neglect that the activities of *"doing good and sharing"* will experience, in spite of any time spent praising and thanking God with our lips. It is though he is saying, "I know some of you think that coming together and singing some songs, listening to the sermon, and tossing money in the plate is enough. It is not. Make sure you take this responsiveness to God for His goodness into your lives every day. That is what God is looking for, and that is what will please Him."

What is really insightful is that this neglect describes exactly how much of the teaching and discussion on worship is taking place today. We can read books about worship techniques, worship songs, Praise and Worship, and how to be a worship leader. We can attend seminars to learn how to plan worship, learn worship history, how to write songs, what technology to use in worship, how to build worship teams, and all about the heart of worship. We have access to videos about ancient worship, future worship, postmodern worship, excellence in worship, styles of worship, drama in worship, dance for worship, liturgical worship, and authentic worship. And every single one of these topics, even if it veers off into other parts of life, comes back to deal with corporate worship as the primary, central aspect of worship. I have said it before and will say it again: this modern discussion on the topic of worship is unbalanced.

This is what the writer of Hebrews warns against, and he balances the praise and thanksgiving of our lips with what? *Action*—doing good and sharing. This is what we tell our kids to do, and maybe as grownups we feel that we have the whole matter under control, but if we do, why the warning in the book of Hebrews?

Many Christians, and worship leaders, worry about worshiping God in the right way (see the discussion on John 4:23-24 in Chapter 5), hoping to please God (or, rather, appease God) with the right song, the right feeling, the right heart, and miss the point of these verses in Hebrews and the point of worship altogether. God will be pleased with our sacrifice—our worship—when we get out there to do good and share. He is pleased with the balanced life of the internal and external being fully integrated. "The human being is, above all else, a worshiping creature whose very act of worship, if it is not perverse, is to establish or deepen belief and to do good."[49]

Hebrews 13:15-16 applies the idea of sacrifice to both aspects of our lives—personally and corporately. We are to sacrifice with our lips of praise, and sacrifice with our activity of good deeds and sharing. One is directed upward to God. The other is directed outward to people. We worship God by balancing the vertical aspects of worship (God to Us, Us to God) with the horizontal aspects (Us to Others, Others to Us). According to these verses in Hebrews, this will please God.

Part III: Corporate Worship

We now move from our discussion of the overall framework for worship—that of a life of worship—to consider what some of the implications might be for the world of corporate worship. The framework, or foundation, we built previously will now help us to build a structure for corporate worship that will hold true against the winds of change and our culture.

We must distinguish, first of all, between a personal life-style of worship and the corporate gathering of the church which we call worship. Part I of this book was to build the Biblical foundation, or frame, for worship as a whole. From this Biblical basis we learned the importance of the internal thoughts and belief systems. We also noted that the internal beliefs manifest themselves in external actions.

Part II was a concentrated discussion about how the internal becomes external in real life, in other words, worship as a life-style. We discovered various aspects of making our lives represent what we believe about worship.

What I mean by a "personal life-style" of worship is a life that reflects the gifts of God in our lives as we use them in love to serve Him and those around us. As mentioned in the chapter on *The Heavens Declare Principle*, each of us worships best as we do what God has created us to be and do.

Ephesians 2:10 is an excellent verse that draws this idea out: *"For we are His workmanship, created in Christ Jesus for good works, which God prepared beforehand, that we should walk in them."* Note that God is the activator of the good works, and we are the responders. Recall that our previous discussions showed that our activity in response to God is a spiritual worship (Romans 12:1). This *individual* experience of responsiveness to God's work in us should be the overall, broad perspective of worship that we have for our **corporate** gatherings to be meaningful.

And so in Part III we consider the ramifications of all that has been said before, and how it might apply in the realm of corporate worship. The daily life of worship and the corporate worship event are distinguishable, yet entirely intertwined. I do not wish to say that one leads to another, as many are fond of saying, yet as we look at worship holistically, we find that these two kinds of worship, or maybe we should call them descriptions, are quite integrated.

"Corporate" worship is specifically that time in which the church, as Christ's body, gathers to recognize God's work in our lives as believers. We gather because God is a relational God, and we are His relational people. We gather as feet and hands and ears and eyes because Christ's body is not complete otherwise. We gather to hear from Him, through His word, and respond to His love, grace, and mercy poured out into our lives.

First Corinthians 12 is a beautiful description of the diversified body worshiping and serving as one body. When we serve faithfully with our gifts, doing our part as God has given us to do, we come alongside others doing the same. We come together in a unified body, living our lives in a personal life-style of worship, to pursue a corporate life of worship. The church (the Body of Christ) is vital to give our individual lives perspective in the larger plan of God in the world.

Corporate worship is the culmination of the gathered Body of Christ that has already been worshiping daily as each Christian has served God by serving others (i.e., the life of worship). The corporate gathering becomes the opportunity to raise a unified voice of thanksgiving and praise to God Who has worked in their midst. It is the response of God's people to His salvation and sanctifying activity in their lives. (All of this takes place in the fullness of the horizontal and vertical aspects of corporate worship that we will consider in the next chapter.)

So, not only do we come to celebrate personal victories and gain support and prayer for personal struggle (as though corporate worship flows from our personal lives), but we also gain perspective from the larger body as to why we are called to live as we do, serving the way we do (as though our personal worship flows from the corporate identity). These two realms of worship are symbiotic. They exist together and flow from one another, and feed each other.

This dual mechanism of worship is evident in Scripture. Note the Psalms, which celebrate the Israelites' walk through the Red Sea (Psalm 77:16-20), or praise God for His activity in the natural world (Psalm 32:6-9). Then turn and read those Psalms in which the author recognizes his personal dependence upon God (Psalm 41) and his connection with God's chosen people (Psalm 47). As a Jew, the psalmist found corporate identity to freely worship individually, and the work of God in the life of Israel gave the nation as a whole a reason to celebrate.

As we move forward, then, keep in mind all of the foundational principles already discussed because they will play a significant role as we build some ideas that flow from them into our settings for corporate worship.

The Four Aspects

Let me re-emphasize that the following discussion is within the context of *corporate worship* and what elements of it we find in Scripture. In other words, what I am discussing here are those things we do when we worship together as a body (congregation, church, small group, etc.). This is the subject matter of Part III of this book.

Let me also remind you that this chapter brings to bear all of the previous chapters of discussion, so it is based upon a larger framework than doing a simple Bible study on worship and relating all of the Old Testament examples of worship in Israel's practice. In fact, my observations will always be tempered through a New Testament filter, especially as found in Paul's epistles and the Hebrew-General epistles (Hebrews through Jude).

Paul is recognized throughout Christendom as the great Apostle to the Gentiles, as he himself claimed and was commissioned to be (see Galatians 1 and 2). That being the case, it seems strange that much teaching on worship has avoided his balanced approach. Rather, worshipers are taught to copy Old Testament Israelite practices and make them contemporary, or to approach worship from Christ's words in John 4:24 which causes a minimalistic theory and method for worship. Let us attempt to go beyond that here.

The Four Aspects of Worship

There are *four aspects* of worship that we, as a church (the Body of Christ), participate in when we come together for corporate worship. These can also be described as four relationships. We must consciously recognize the existence of these relationships and understand that each one is active within the worship experience. If not, we will miss something that the Lord may want to teach us. We must open our eyes to see, and our ears to hear God's voice in the various ways in which He speaks through His word and through His people.

Biblically, worship can be seen to have four aspects, or dimensions, or relationships: *two vertical* and *two horizontal*. By the *vertical* dimension of corporate worship, I mean the relationship that exists between God and His people. These two vertical aspects can be described as follows: *God to the People* and *the People to God*. I also like to make it more personal by stating: *God to Us* and *Us to God*. These are the most commonly recognized aspects of worship, with considerable emphasis in current popular discussions on the idea of the people to God.

By the *horizontal* dimension of corporate worship, I mean the relationship between the people and each other. The two horizontal aspects can be identified this way: *Others to Us* and *Us to Others*. Most people generally hold these two aspects at arms length, though Biblically they are key elements of public worship. We find this true when considering the aspects of worship in Colossians 3:12-17:

> *So, as those who have been chosen of God, holy and beloved, put on a heart of compassion, kindness, humility, gentleness and patience; bearing with one another, and forgiving each other, whoever has a complaint against anyone; just as the Lord forgave you, so also should you.*
>
> *Beyond all these things put on love, which is the perfect bond of unity. Let the peace of Christ rule in your hearts, to which indeed you were called in one body; and be thankful. Let the word of Christ richly dwell within you, with all wisdom teaching and admonishing one another with psalms and hymns*

*and spiritual songs, singing with thankfulness in your
hearts to God.*
    *Whatever you do in word or deed, do all in the
name of the Lord Jesus, giving thanks through Him to
God the Father.*

Note the inclusiveness and sense of community that are
infused into these words.   This worship, this life as
Christians, is an effort of "we" rather than "I."
    So the four aspects in succession are: ***God to Us, Us to
God, Others to Us,*** and ***Us to Others.***   This is a
deliberate and balanced approach to corporate worship:

Vertical relationships
* God to Us
* Us to God

Horizontal relationships
* Us to Others
* Others to Us

As pastors, worship leaders and worship planners, we
must take each of these into consideration and realize that
people will respond to each one differently.   Some will
respond to one aspect, or relationship, one week and a
different aspect another week. This is the result of God's
Spirit working in them, as well as through us as we plan and
execute the plan. It would be appropriate, then, to have each
one represented well in each service.   This must be
deliberate and well thought out.
    As worshipers, we must allow God to speak to us, or
through us, as He desires. Worship is to be fully active and
our physical participation is vital (see Romans 12:1-2).
When we are aware of each of these four relational aspects of

corporate worship we will enjoy it more, and experience the fullness of what God intended.

All four are significant and have their place in worship, yet I was reminded recently that one of these four aspects is critical—in fact absolutely essential—for the others to even exist. I have placed it in my list as first, or *primary*.

Keep the Main Thing the Main Thing!!

God to Us. This is where all worship begins and ends. The other aspects of worship, whether personal and private or corporate and public, are dependent upon this one. In fact, our whole lifestyle of worship is dependent upon God's communication of His love to us. God has spoken through His word, and through the Living Word, Jesus Christ. God has revealed Himself to us through the Bible, and ultimately (and most intimately) through Jesus: the God-man, deity embodied in human flesh. That is what *Immanuel* communicates to us, "*God with us.*"

The primary method in which God communicates is through the word we call the Bible. Paul encouraged Timothy to publicly read Scripture as an important aspect of corporate life, "*Give attention to the public reading of Scripture, to exhortation and to teaching*" (1 Timothy 4:13). This can happen in a multitude of ways including unison reading, antiphonal reading (back and forth, or call and answer), dramatized readings, memorized presentations, Scripture put to music, and more. I recall a very effective instance in which a man quoted the entire book of Philippians (from memory!) including all the emotions and concern that Paul included in his words. This presentation is still remembered as one of the most effective presentations of Scripture many of those present had ever experienced. In this way—through His word—God is communicating to us.

Why is this idea of **God to us** primary to our worship? Because every other aspect of our worship is a **response** to this one, and responding to God is what the life of worship is all about. As Allen and Borror point out, "Worship is revelation and response...Hear the Word—receive! Do the Word—respond! Worship means to respond to God. If we fail to respond, worship has probably not occurred."[50]

We respond in praise and thanksgiving (Us to God) during our worship, and in the popular phraseology "ascribe worth to God." We hear from others, and allow them to serve us (Others to Us), because they are responding to the gifts He has given (both the gift of salvation and the gifts of the spirit as taught in such places as Ephesians 4 and First Corinthians 12). We speak and serve others (Us to Others), in response to the gifts God has given us. Always remember, *"We love because He first loved us!"* (1 John 4:19)

If this is true, how is it that so many discussions on worship begin with the idea of **Us to God**, rather than the concept of **God to us**, and seem to never get around to even considering any of the other aspects of a balanced view of worship? We worry so much about doing the right style of music, singing the right lyrics, engaging the "youth" while not alienating the "older folk"—but I am not sure that I have ever heard a discussion that asked, "How can we best listen to God during our service?" Or, "How can we create an atmosphere that will not inhibit God's voice?"

Now I am not calling for some quasi-mystical approach to worship planning and the worship experience, though worship may have some mystical aspects. What I am calling for is that we **Keep the Main Thing the Main Thing!** God has spoken, and is still speaking, but we do not stop talking long enough to listen. This is because we get caught up in "us" and "we" and "I." The service is for "us" to worship God. "We" need to do this for worship. "I" must get that out of worship. All of these kinds of comments betray the reality that the focus is not on God, but upon our own experience. In typical fashion in the human experience, we have moved God to a secondary position and ourselves up front (please reference Isaiah 53:6 and consider whether we should apply it to our lives both before and after salvation).

In some church traditions, hearing God's voice is built-in to the fabric of worship. Take the Eastern Orthodox tradition with its icons and incense, and the mysterious way (at least to the Western mind) in which worship is practiced. Their focus is on how God has communicated to us as humans. The icons (simply visual representations of important people and events) remind them of His voice throughout the centuries—what He said and how He said it. They seem to be intent on hearing what *God* is saying, rather than always speaking themselves to make certain that God is hearing what *they* are saying.

Other traditions hear the voice of God through the pastor's sermon. I wonder if those of us who preach realize that we are often the voice of God to our congregations? How would our sermons be different if this was on our mind as we prepared and delivered **HIS** message, rather than our own thoughts about His message?

Ultimately, worship is a complex thing that must ebb and flow with the needs of the congregation, the gifts of the leaders *and* the message sent by God. We must never lose sight of the fact that without His message, without the Gospel, without God having first communicated His love to us we would have no reason to do or say anything else.

How We Respond

The second relationship that we experience in worship has already been mentioned. It is the vertical relationship of us focusing upward to God. In this we do ascribe worth to Him (Psalm 66:1-4). We thank Him and praise Him for Who He is and what He does (Psalm 66:5-7). Together we focus our hearts and minds on God the Father, His Son and the Spirit. Paul says that we do this *"with one accord and with one voice"* (Romans 15:6) as a community. We are communicating: *Us to God.*

By its very nature, this second of the vertical aspects of worship must be subordinate to the first. We must consider this a response to God's communication of Himself (condescension) to us. Scripture is full of examples that show this aspect of worship being one of response to Him: response to His activity in the world, His intervention in human events, and His unfailing love and mercy.

How has the current discussion on worship become so unbalanced? Why has this secondary aspect of worship been the primary focus for so long? I believe there are several reasons.

First of all, modern discussions of worship focus primarily on the public worship service. In fact, worship, in these discussions, can be defined as "a group event sponsored by the church in which we gather to focus upward toward God." Thus follows the inevitable discussion on music, style, preaching techniques, multi-media, etc.

Unfortunately, beneath this focus on the event is an absence of theological understanding and a continuation of man's greatest problem: pride. We like to focus on ourselves, and while we claim to discuss "worship" in the context of "ascribing worth to God," in reality we are discussing ourselves: what we like, what style fits us, what style fits the seeker, what felt-needs must be met, what structure works best in our culture, and the like. These things are not about God; they are about us. This, in large part, is the result of misunderstanding Jesus' words in John 4:23-24 as discussed in Chapter 5.

Another problem, as I see it, is that too many well-meaning musicians have expressed their "philosophy" of ministry without a good theological foundation to build upon. They have ventured into theological discourse without the tools or background to do so accurately and fully. There are reasons that men and women in previous centuries are considered "giants" of the faith, especially the great Christian musicians and composers. They understood the Bible and theology better than the average layman, as well as their own craft. For example, did you know that J.S. Bach's library consisted largely of several versions of the Bible and Martin Luther's writings? During that time, this was considered a huge private library, and Bach was thoroughly familiar with each and every volume.

Consider other composers found in the pages of the hymnal: Isaac Watts, John and Charles Wesley...all great hymn-writers, yes, but well-grounded theologians first. In the late Twentieth Century this balance of rock-solid theology and well-crafted music was sorely missing, and for the most part continues to be absent today. The worship music of the last fifty years is theologically thin and often poorly written music as well. It is no wonder the church is so unbalanced in this area. Worship thought and practice has left the foundation of Scripture and good doctrine for the experience of how church "feels" to the individual worshiper.

Horizontal Relationships

The third relationship we find in corporate worship, that is often overlooked, is the horizontal dimension of *Us speaking to Others*. In this dimension we share our faith and encourage other believers. This is communicated in many of the songs we sing, although we often sing right through and miss the point. For example, as we sing: "Come, Christians Join to Sing" we are inviting one another to worship:

Come, Christians, join to sing; Alleluia! Amen!
Loud Praise to Christ our King; Alleluia! Amen!
Let all, with heart and voice,
Before His throne rejoice;
Praise is His gracious choice: Alleluia! Amen![51]

The popular chorus "Come, Now is the Time to Worship" has the same message:

Come, now is the time to worship.
Come, now is the time to give your heart.
Come, just as you are to worship.
Come, just as you are before your God. Come![52]

Try having two (or more) parts of your congregation face each other when singing a song like this, actually inviting each other to worship. Colossians 3:16 is full of references to various aspects of us speaking and singing to one another for teaching and encouragement, "*with all wisdom teaching and admonishing one another.*"

Of course, balance must be the main emphasis in planning corporate worship. A congregation could easily focus too much time and energy on these horizontal aspects and completely miss the fact that God is trying to speak. We must remember that our loving response to God, although directed toward others (both believer and unbeliever), is still a response to God. The motivation must not be to feel better about ourselves, or to try and get someone to like us better. We respond from a thankful heart out of a desire to honor God in all that we do. Read Colossians 3:17 again! "*And whatever you do in word or deed, do all in the name of the Lord Jesus, giving thanks through Him to God the Father.*"

The fourth aspect of corporate worship is quite interrelated with the third. It is the other horizontal dimension in which we are the receivers rather than the givers. This is when ***Others speak to Us***. The sermon is really only one example of this aspect of worship relationships. We are on the receiving end of admonition, encouragement, teaching, story-telling, and learning about God, His work, and our response to Him from many directions. This can come to us through the pastor, a testimony, the choir, a soloist, our neighbor in the pew, or our Sunday School teacher. It might even be a well-timed comment from a friend in the hallway. Again, Colossians 3:16 is a perfect reference for this when read through the eyes of a receiver. This type of communication is horizontal, and part of the bigger picture of balanced worship.

One Way Worship

One of the ideas in modern worship theory that I question is the thought that worship takes place primarily in one direction. That is, when people teach or write about worship the reference is generally to that aspect of worship in which ***we*** direct our thoughts and focus ***toward God***. You have probably heard it put this way: "When we worship, we are ascribing to God His worth. It can be defined as worth-ship."

I am not saying that this idea of worship is not important, because it is. It does seem shallow to me, because I am responding to a lack of balance, as well as the misconception or misappropriation of defining worship in a limited way such as "ascribing worth." I would simply like to see more balance and a more accurate representation of what Scripture actually teaches concerning what we do when we worship, both individually and as a corporate body.

Are we to say that when we ascribe value to our spouse or child, or even to a cherished possession, we are "worshiping" that thing more than God? Obviously not, but when have you ever heard someone talk about the varying degrees of "ascribing worth" in the course of our lives? I ascribe worth to my wife, my children, my golf clubs, and my house, for they truly are "worth" something to me. Apparently, in applying this definition of worship and taking the logic of the argument to its conclusion, I am "worshiping" my wife, my children, my golf clubs and my house. Does this really mean that I do not "worship" God? That I do not "ascribe worth" to Him appropriately? Or, rather, does it mean that we need to think more clearly about this definition and refine what these ideas mean?

I think you get my point. Worship is more than "worthship," and a discussion that focuses so narrowly on that one component is simply not balanced. It is too narrow and confining.

Realignment

By realigning our ideas and practice of corporate worship to fully reflect all four of the key relationships discussed above, we will come to find a breadth and depth of worship we have never experienced. Relational community will become ever richer as we all realize that by serving others, and allowing them to serve us, we truly worship God as a body and express a balanced worship with all of our being. John expresses this communal living beautifully in his epistle:

> *Beloved, let us love one another, for love is from God; and everyone who loves is born of God and knows God. The one who does not love does not know God, for God is love. By this the love of God was manifested in us, that God has sent His only begotten Son into the world so that we might live through Him. In this is love, not that we loved God, but that He loved us and sent His Son to be the propitiation for our sins.*

Beloved, if God so loved us, we also ought to love one another. (1 John 4:7-11)

Mutual love and service for one another is the key to meaningful worship within the community. The members of the Body of Christ must actively serve one another in order to fulfill the mission of worship God has placed upon the church—a mission of love and service. According to the Apostle John, as quoted above, we are following the very example of God in loving others this way. What better way to honor God, to worship Him, than to follow His example closely?

So let us worship fully in a balanced way that recognizes God's communication to us and our response to Him. The primary aspect of corporate worship is God revealing Himself to us—***God to Us***. We, as His people, respond to God in three ways: ***Us to God, Us to Others***, and ***Others to Us***. God has spoken to us. May we appropriately respond in all the variety and diversity that we as His gifted people represent.

Transitions and Distractions

I currently live in the state of Michigan. As I write, we are in the midst of the second of two seasons we have each year. I realize that many of you have the traditional four-season year, which generally includes Winter, Spring, Summer, and Autumn. However, in Michigan (and from what I understand in several other North American geographical locations) we only have two seasons: 1) Winter, and 2) Road Construction season. I suppose we could even simplify that by calling these two seasons: 1) Construction Season, and 2) Non-construction Season. Either way, I think you understand my meaning.

Along with the usual telltale signs of the season, such as slower traffic, warning signs, and flashing lights, there are also the men and women standing around watching other men and women do the actual work. There are the big "tractors" (strictly present for the entertainment of my young son), the cranes and dirt-movers, and the inevitable orange barrels squeezing traffic into one lane. And we must not forget the bright orange signs, which remind us that speeding in a construction zone will earn the double-bonus fine!

Eventually, after longer than predicted and spending more money than planned, a new road is finished, or an old one re-surfaced. We anticipate the days when, at 70MPH we can ride along in comfort, no bumps, no worries, no signs, and no threats—only the open road!!

On a recent voyage into the far reaches of our state, I found myself in the middle of a construction zone (had I known it was there, I would have avoided it). Finding plenty of time to reflect on the fact that I was working on this book,

I pondered the "lessons of the road" so-to-speak. As I lost myself in thought, traffic moved along and eventually I found myself once again on an open road traveling full speed. No major hitches, and I was on my way.

A little later in my journey, I found myself in what appeared to be another construction site, on a road that had just recently been widened. The difference here was that the construction was complete, and other than a dark black surface of the road, bright yellow and white lines, and new grass coming through the dirt at the side of the road, everything was smooth sailing. The crews were gone, the work was done, all was well.

Then I hit it!! At least I thought I hit something. It was abrupt, and shook the steering wheel in my hands. (If you saw my truck, you would know why this is slightly alarming!) I thought I might have run over that unsuspecting chicken that was crossing to the other side of the road, but as I glanced in my rearview mirror, I saw no dead chicken. Then, I realized what had happened. It was not the chicken, or a bunny, or something previously hit by another speeding vehicle. It was the connection of the newer road to the older one.

Get the picture? You know what I am talking about. When a road is repaired or re-surfaced it must ultimately connect to an older section of the road. It is really evident here in Michigan, because as the black surfaces of the new roads are weathered they fade to a dull gray. When a new, black surface comes against an older, gray surface it is pretty obvious.

It is obvious due to the color change, but sometimes it is also obvious because the crew working the project was unable to connect, or transition, the two surfaces in a smooth, unnoticeable way. Sometimes there is a ridge, or a slight bump, or maybe the connection is a bit rough. This was what I experienced when I thought I had hit something.

As I reflected, I realized that the first road crew I had encountered had done an excellent job with the transition from new road to old road. You will note in my description above that as I pondered my thoughts that day I suddenly realized that I was on an open road again. There had been a transition, for the road had changed color, but I had not felt the change from a dip, bump or any other abnormality in the road. It was a ***smooth transition*** from one to the other.

Perspective on Transitions

I could not help but put things in perspective for this chapter. ***Corporate worship, or a Public worship service, at its very core, consists of various elements (songs, prayers, Scripture, drama, sermon, etc.), which are connected together by a series of transitions***. And, just like my experience on the road, these transitions can be quite "bumpy" and rough, or they can take place without anyone noticing.

Of course, we would prefer to execute a smooth, flawless transition each and every time during each and every service. A breakdown during a transition is one of the most disruptive things that can happen during a service. The thought and feeling of the moment can be damaged and difficult to re-gain. Smooth, effective transitions can help build a public worship service toward a desired goal: the majesty of God, a listening ear to the Spirit, the wonder of the cross of Christ.

When a ***transition*** crumbles it immediately takes on a life of its own and becomes the nemesis of corporate worship. It becomes a ***distraction***. This metamorphosis is not optional when a transition breaks down. Someone, somewhere in that service is now distracted from the song, or prayer, or sermon, or comment, or worst of all, away from the internal work of the Spirit. None of us can prevent all mistakes, but we can try to minimize distractions. Let me share my thoughts about this.

The Most Important Element

Let me start by asking this question: What is the most important element of a Worship Service? By element I mean the different aspects or pieces that are combined to make the whole service. Would you say the sermon is the most important? Or maybe Scripture reading? How about prayer? Maybe music deserves high marks? Talk to any room full of people and the debate would be endless. I have found it interesting that there is such a diverse range of opinions on the matter, yet when I have taught on the topic of worship there is one element that never receives attention.

Notice that my initial question was very specific. I did not ask about the most important element or idea of *worship* as a topic, but of a ***Worship Service***. The question is one of a practical nature concerning corporate worship, as opposed to a philosophical or theological perspective. The analysis of a Worship Service on this level is vital as our congregations come together for the purpose of experiencing God through song, sermon, prayer and other ways of engaging our hearts and minds. Does this clarification to the question change your answer in any way?

Arguments are plentiful for the inclusion and importance of Scripture, the sermon, music, prayer and other elements in our Worship Services. Our weekly gatherings as the Body of Christ are significant opportunities to hear from God in various ways. But what is the connecting thread? What element do we all notice if it does not happen, or work well, but when it is properly executed we do not notice at all?

Having read this far, you already know my answer. What is the most important element of a Worship Service? The transition. You might think I am a little crazy now. What do

I see that is so vital about a transition? Better yet, what do I find that is so spiritual about a transition? Well, I am glad you asked; so let me explain what I mean.

Another analogy I like to use is this: transitions are the links of the chain. In the course of corporate worship, *when moving from one element to another, something happens* (you either notice it or you do not) and *that something is a transition*. If one of those "links" breaks, it is obvious to everyone. When the "link" holds strong, it is as though it does not even exist. Are you moving from a song to a prayer? There you find a transition. Moving from the Scripture reading to the sermon? Another transition. Moving from songs, to announcements, to more songs? More transitions.

Consider this: a successfully executed Worship Service is a service of successful transitions. Good transitions lead to minimal distractions from the established flow of a service. Bad transitions are distractions that even great music or excellent sermons have difficulty overcoming. That is what makes transitions, good transitions, so important to our corporate Worship Services.

Now, I certainly do not want to undervalue the quality of the other elements of worship. A poorly performed song can be a fatal distraction. A sermon that does not communicate with people at their level will lead to wandering minds and disinterest. An unprepared testimony can soon become a meandering soliloquy. My point is that our services deserve as much time, energy and thought put into transitions as we do the other elements.

Serving a new church as Pastor of Music and Worship, my first order of business was to analyze the Worship Services as they had been done prior to my arrival. I did this using videos of various services and timing each element as it passed. What I discovered was that we needed to concentrate on transitions and the flow of the services.

Believe it or not, we made no significant changes in the style of worship (we did not even add any new songs) for at least six months. But, when we began to work on transitions and flow, the results were readily noticeable. Within just a month or two, we were able to draw together the loose ends and begin to create an atmosphere that minimized distractions and helped people focus on the theme of the day. Our services began to be holistic events, rather than a series of unrelated activities taking place in the same room.

Transitions are one of the most vital elements in our corporate Worship Services. Do not ignore them or underestimate their value. Someone needs to be aware of them and think them through *before* they happen. This is the best way to ensure their successful deployment and smooth sailing from week to week.

The Role of the worship leader

These thoughts about transitions and distractions lead me to what I consider to be the most important role of the worship leader. Before I share my view, let me review some of the prevailing ideas that circulate about who the worship leader is and what he or she does.

Of course, in each church someone inevitably fulfills the role of worship leader. Who is that in your congregation? A paid staff person? A volunteer? The pastor? An associate pastor? Regardless, the individual has a vital part to play in the unfolding of the corporate worship setting within any congregation. Following is a short list of some popular views.

First, there is one theory circulating that turns the title "worship leader" on its head and suggests that this person is the "lead worshiper." In other words, it is assumed that this person should have a heart and attitude of worship both individually and in front of the corporate body and that this qualifies him or her to then lead the worship of the congregation.

Second, there is the theory that the "worship leader" is really the "song leader." Within this realm the person only leads the songs, especially since the rest of the elements of the service are not really considered "worship." Other individuals handle other aspects of the service (i.e., announcements, pastoral prayer, offertory, Scripture reading, etc.).

Third, some suggest that the "worship leader" is the pastor. Why? Well...because he's the pastor. The pastor's primary responsibility is the planning and execution of the Sunday Service, so regardless of who else does the planning, song leading, etc. the pastor is the "worship leader."

Fourth, how about the idea that the "worship leader" is a Team? The expressed purpose of this approach is to avoid drawing attention to any single person. A "Worship Team" is developed to facilitate and lead the worship, as well at times to help with the planning. This also allows for shared responsibility.

Fifth, another possibility is that the "worship leader" is actually the "worship planner." He or she is responsible to plan the various elements of the service, but does not necessarily lead the congregation in any way on Sunday. This allows for a wide use of gifted individuals in the leading of the services.

Sixth, in some primarily denominational settings, the Organist is the "worship leader." There may be someone up front "leading" the songs, but he or she is actually following the Organist—not vice versa. In this model the Organist segues between elements of the service, sets the tempo of the songs, and can even help the pastor realize that he has gone too long by moving to his seat at the organ at the appointed time!

There may be more theories, but I think you see that the role of the worship leader is neither well-defined nor commonly understood. If we were to think through each of the above "theories" we could actually make a case that there is merit for each one. The "worship leader" should be a worshiper, and often their primary activity is leading songs. He is often the pastor, who at least sets the spiritual tone for the service. In some settings a Team approach works great, and sometimes the planner of the services is gifted in planning, but not in leading a group in public. There are even instances in which the Organist, or another musician, should take the lead role in the service as is fitting for the moment. All of these ideas work, in the appropriate setting and circumstances.

Let me share another idea with you about the role of the worship leader. Even if one of the above methods is predominant, what I would like to suggest actually functions alongside each. I would like to suggest that one of the worship leader's primary roles is to **gather distractions**. Yes, you read that correctly—**gather distractions**. I can hear you now, "What is this guy talking about? He has gone off the deep end." Just keep reading and I will explain.

The first part of this chapter explains the importance of transitions in worship. Transitioning from song to song, song to prayer, prayer to sermon, sermon to song, etc. can make or break the atmosphere of worship. Muff up a transition and the congregation can lose focus. Fall apart moving from one song to another and the joy of the moment is replaced with frustration and embarrassment.

Gathering distractions is another form of dealing with transitions. A broken transition is a distraction to the congregation. A worship leader must anticipate this and do all that is humanly possible to avoid distractions that will interrupt the congregation's focus. He must gather the distractions to himself. **In many ways that means the**

worship leader must be full of distractions in order to provide for the congregation to have few distractions.

As a worship leader plans and prepares for an upcoming corporate gathering, there are many methods that can be used to minimize distractions. It is in forethought and planning that many distractions can be avoided. Details for the transitions can be noted and practiced.

One way to do this is to visualize the service before it happens. Will Mrs. Smith be able to get up to the piano without tripping on those cords? Do the Deacons know when the Offering will be taken and do they have people ready to do that? Is it too warm or cold in the sanctuary? Does the choir have enough time to sit down between their two songs, or should they remain standing? Can the congregation hear the speaker and singers well enough? How is the lighting?

I have used this technique of visualizing the service before it happens over and over again with great success. The more complicated the service, the more time spent visualizing. I have found that it helps to go into the sanctuary (or gym, or cafeteria, or wherever you do worship) and "see" the event happening. I am not suggesting some mystical, new age vision-seeking. It is more like rehearsing an important conversation before it even happens. What are you going to say? How should you say it? Where should you be when you say it? When should the choir move? Does the pastor enter from backstage, the first pew or seated on the platform?

Practice

Well, how is this done? How does the worship leader plan a service with good transitions and be sure that it all goes smoothly? This is what we want, but how do we make it happen?

Practice. You heard me: ***Practice***! Especially for the musicians. Spend time rehearsing prior to the service (during the week, on Saturday, etc.). I have often led rehearsals, in which we have spent more time rehearsing transitions from song to song, or song to prayer, or Scripture reading to sermon, or hundreds of other combinations than the time we have spent actually rehearsing the music. That is how important transitions are, and the only way to get better at them is to rehearse them. The leader of the service must think them through (beforehand), and communicate to those involved what the transitions should look like. Then, the participants must work through each transition to be sure everyone knows what to expect. Doing this will remove the possibility of a "train wreck," as some of my associates have called muffed-up transitions.

I can assure you with a great deal of confidence that if you spend time each week for the next month practicing the transitions found in your plan for worship, that by the end of the month your worship services will seem to be going much, much smoother. Why?? Because they ***are*** going much, much smoother!! Then, keep on practicing and see what will happen!

Context and Planning

When viewed through the lens of spiritual giftedness, public worship becomes a unique experience. It is unique to each and every local congregation. As a microcosm of the Body of Christ, each local congregation—from the megachurch to the house church—has a special set of Spirit-empowered gifts within it. Discovering and using these gifts in public worship will add a wonderful variety to the worship of any group. And variety is exactly what God intended.

I can foresee readers assuming they know what the "gifts" are for use in corporate worship: preaching and teaching, singing and instrumental gifts primarily. There may be a few others thrown in, but when it comes to public worship, these few are what come to most minds. This is, however, a fairly narrow understanding of the use of God's gifts within public worship, and it is the result of a pattern established by some apparently successful ministries throughout the years.

Variety is really not what we find when we view the worship practices throughout North American churches today, and many modern Western churches in general. By and large, we find an almost exact duplicate from one church to the next, at varying levels of competency, regardless of denomination or political leanings. The players and preachers are different, some of the songs and messages are different, attire may be radically different, yet there is an amazing and utter lack in variety.

Franchising

Worship, in today's American Evangelical culture, has essentially been franchised. Some large, and apparently successful (they are large, are they not?) churches cause a stir and a sensation. People do not just attend there, they flock there by the thousands. Pastors and musicians in smaller churches look around, hear the buzz created (even among their own congregation), and wonder what they can do to "compete" (a classic American response when someone appears to be doing better than you). These small church leaders attend the Big Church Conferences and learn the Big Church Techniques in order to utilize them in their own church setting, thus entering the franchising cycle. The best of the best of these franchises propagate themselves exponentially so that their methods for pragmatic success can be seen throughout the land, or even the world. They sponsor the conferences, write the books, sell the study materials, and generally have a rousing good time duplicating themselves.

Since public worship is the most noticeable (visible) of what these franchise organizations do, we end up with a bunch of not-quite-so-polished copies. Songs and music styles are duplicated. Sermons and sermon styles take a "fresh" twist. Décor and attire become "friendly" to the un-churched. Even vision statements and mission statements begin to have conceptual similarities, if not outright "copy-and-paste" duplication.

Is the church universal really meant to have such limited options in its practice of public worship? Are churches that just do "hymns" really irrelevant? Are "contemporary" churches really speaking to the needs of the age? Do the proponents of "blended" or "mixed" worship styles actually bridge the gap that presumably exists between the contemporary and the traditional?

I believe the answers to these questions are quite dependent upon something that a "franchise" cannot take into consideration. Have you noticed that once a fast-food chain has discovered what works, the duplication of its food becomes standard whether you buy your sandwich in

Florida, Wisconsin or Arizona? Although prices vary by region, you can trust that the burger and fries you buy on vacation will be almost an exact copy of what you get in your own hometown. The same is true of franchised church methods: *the success is in the accuracy and duplication of the method.* If it fails in your church, the plan must not have been followed properly. After all, it works for the Big Church!!

Ministry Context

What these carbon-copied methods fail to address adequately is the issue of *ministry context.* What I mean by this is the special geographical, historical, political, sociological, ecclesiastical, and theological characteristics of each and every particular occurrence of the Body of Christ known as a local church.

Context is important and we learn about the concept when we begin to read at an early age. It is what helps us get an overall understanding of what a particular paragraph or passage is about in relationship to the whole chapter or book. In fact, it is defined in the dictionary as the "related or adjoining passages of a book." Often, by understanding the context, one can even decipher the meaning of unfamiliar words and ideas.

Somehow, though most of us are familiar with the idea of context, we often fail to apply the relationships of context in other areas of life. We may overhear a comment from someone involved in a conversation, and by not understanding the context of the *entire* conversation; we can misinterpret the one short phrase we heard. That is what we mean when something is taken "out of context."

Most often as Christians we hear criticism (and voice criticism!) when a passage of Scripture is "taken out of context." What is generally meant is that the interpretation of a verse or passage is mishandled due to a lack of consideration of the larger chapter, book, author, literary style, or even the Testament in which it is found. The "related and adjoining passages" have been ignored and the interpreter uses the passage out of convenience and the need to prove a point, rather than faithfully using methods of proper interpretation to draw the meaning from the passage itself.

I have found it helpful at times to discuss worship and ministry with this in mind. One of the responsibilities of a worship leader, pastor, or worship planner is to understand the **context** within which he or she is planning and leading. The need to understand the context of ministry is, of course, true of any Church leader in every area of ministry, but we are talking about worship so let me narrow my comments in that direction.

Contextual worship planning

The craft of planning and leading worship is one that is pastoral by nature. Although many worship planners and leaders do not hold pastoral **titles**, what they do actually fulfills an influential **role** in equipping the saints and building up the Body of Christ (and we will look into this more concretely in the next chapter. See also Ephesians 4:11-16). In so doing, they must make specific efforts to understand the context within which they are ministering.

There is a crucial balance that must be sought and maintained in the contextual framework of any ministry. For the worship leader, a study and appreciation of the congregation's history is significant and must include both musical and theological elements. He or she must also strive to comprehend the current perspectives of the congregation on both theology and music. Gaining this knowledge can be done both formally and informally. Administering surveys to members of the congregation can give someone a good idea of the congregation's leanings in musical style, volume, instrumentation, etc. The church's constitution is also a good place to discover the theological idiosyncrasies of the denomination or local body.

Informally, smaller meetings can be arranged with interested individuals for friendly discussion of what is expected, liked and desired. "Question and Answer" opportunities in Sunday School classes are another good tool. Regular conversations with individuals can have a specific agenda that will help to bring clarity to the discussion. The best way to get information is to ask questions. The more targeted the questions, the more specific information one will acquire.

The other part of understanding the context of the ministry is knowing how the congregation needs to go. In other words, as a person in a pastoral role, the worship leader is responsible to help the congregation grow. Understanding their likes and dislikes helps us understand what makes them comfortable. Understanding how they need to grow is knowing what might make them uncomfortable.

Worship leading is about LEADING. Sometimes a congregation must be led through songs and worship styles that are well-known. They are comfortable. At other times, they must be led through songs and worship styles that are not-so-comfortable. The songs are new, the music style is different, and drama or other creative material is inserted into the worship experience. This will stretch people and help broaden their faith.

THE KEY IS BALANCE. No one wants to be uncomfortable all the time. And, no one should be left comfortable all the time. *The worship leader can only strike this balance by understanding the context* within which he or she is ministering. Get to know the people in the congregation. Listen to them and take their advice. Lead them and help them grow.

Gifts and corporate worship

So, in regards to how God has gifted a particular congregation, understanding the context will also help one to see the possible variety available from within the congregation. What happens, for example, when a local church finds itself without accompaniment (no guitarist, no pianist, no organist)? Certainly *a cappella* singing is one solution, but what if there is truly no one even gifted enough to lead any songs? What if the meeting must be held quietly due to persecution or privacy? Remove music from the public worship gathering and what do you have? Well, I guess you only have a sermon, a prayer, some Scripture reading—and, of course, the offering!!

Unfortunately, most churchgoers and probably many worship planners and pastors have never seriously considered this, and then thought forward enough to consider what other gifts God may have given people within their congregation. If the electricity went out, surely church must be postponed or cancelled!

Let me throw out some ideas. This is a list of elements that can be incorporated into corporate worship that will add both variety and depth. This list recognizes the unending diversity that God gives in the midst of congregations to spread His word. When we let go of the narrow assumption that worship is only about us praising God, and realize that corporate worship is us listening to God and then responding (the Four Aspects), then wonderful things can, and do, happen.

I have not personally experienced or incorporated all of these ideas in worship. I draw this list from books, conversations, lectures, magazines and other sources. The list is not comprehensive and is intended to get your own creative juices flowing. So here it is:

A few ideas for Corporate Worship...
- Extended sessions of prayer (corporate, small group, individual)
- Five minutes of silent prayer
- Live painting during the sermon or Bible Study
- Feet washing
- An "interruptible" sermon (to allow spontaneous questions and comments)
- Testimonials on a specific subject (God's provision; Lessons from my Prayer Closet; etc.)
- Dance, Mime, movement
- Simultaneous translation into foreign languages
- Simultaneous signing for the deaf
- Interspersed periods of silence/quiet
- Reading an entire book of Scripture (Reader's Theatre or memorized)
- Drama or skits
- Thematic prayer or Scripture reading (or both!)
- Requests for assistance and immediate response from other attendees
- Interviews with "Senior" Christians
- Interviews with "new" Christians
- Interviews with children
- Reading of prepared or original poetry
- Reading from C.S. Lewis' "Chronicles of Narnia" or other Christian authors
- Readings from the Church fathers
- Listening to the rain
- Listening, just listening...
- Sentence prayers of thanksgiving

- Use acoustic instruments like strings, or woodwinds
- Have a service with no sound system
- Let the youth plan and lead the service
- Let a children's group plan and lead the service
- Include every age represented in your congregation on the worship team
- Walk through the church building, as a congregation, and pray
- Walk around your neighborhood, on Sunday morning, and pray
- Participate in a "Sermon Swap" with several other pastors in the area—each of you preaching at another church. Do this once a month for a whole year.
- When planning worship, finish the question, "I wonder what would happen if...?"
- Split up the sermon into parts and intersperse music to match the points of the sermon
- If you are a liturgical church, ask a non-liturgical worship leader to lead worship for you
- If you are a non-liturgical church, ask a liturgical worship leader to lead worship for you
- Be creative!

Some of you reading this might be saying, "Right. Like I am going to lead that kind of worship or do **that** in my worship service." Well, that is the whole point. Within each local representation of the Body of Christ different gifts reside within people who can lead or perform these things (and many, many others) with competence and in excellence. It is not a good idea to have someone read Scripture, or a selection from St. Augustine, if they read in a monotone voice. If, however, someone has the ability to read with passion and style, a passage can become suddenly alive for the hearers.

Do not fall into the trap that you, as the pastor, worship leader, or worship planner must be an expert in whatever element might be planned. Mold the planning of corporate worship around the expertise and giftedness of those within your congregation, allowing the context of the congregation to dictate the style of worship. This will allow the local Body of Christ to operate as God has structured it.

This does not sound easy, does it? In fact, it sounds like a lot of work. It takes time to think about it, plan it, discover the possibilities within the congregation, tap into the willingness of those who have various gifts, help train and focus their abilities, etc, etc. Well, yes, it takes a lot of work. Take it on, or do not take it at all. If it is worth the work and commitment involved, then it is really worth it and demands the best of our time, energy, and talents.

A Final Point on Personal Context

This leads to a final point: *in many ways the worship leader must please himself last.* The reason I say this is in response to a misguided theory of worship leading which says that a worship leader must be the "lead worshiper." I understand the thought behind this idea, that a worship leader must worship God deeply and intimately in order to lead others in worship. This is absolutely true in his or her own lifestyle of worship. However, in corporate worship the way this is often interpreted is that many worship leaders plan worship that *they* like, and songs which minister to them *personally*. When this happens, many congregations watch the "lead worshiper" doing his or her thing, but participate in very little worship as a community. The leader has ignored the context of the ministry in lieu of his or her personal context, and ends up doing very little leading after all.

Mark S. Sooy

So when we plan and lead worship, we must look at the "related and adjoining" elements that can give us an overall perspective on the people within the ministry. When we do this, we are honoring those who have called us, both learning from them and leading them. It's a "win-win" situation all around.

The Worship Leader: Pastor, Theologian, Musician

By now you have already seen and read several references I have made to the issue of leadership of corporate worship. I would like to spend time now giving some breadth to my comments and filling in details that might otherwise be missed, for in these times of continuing adjustment and flux in corporate worship we are in dire need of qualified leadership.

I believe I have made a serious case for corporate worship being one of the many avenues to challenge and inspire the church, as well as to teach and admonish. No doubt, corporate worship is about our thankful praise to the God of gods and Lord of lords, but only in part. It is, in a more balanced approach, an interplay of the *God to Us* and *Us to God* vertical aspects and the *Us to Others* and *Others to Us* horizontal aspects. That means there is much more to leading worship than what is commonly thought.

I want to ask before you read further that you read this chapter in its entirety. Some of what I say may seem provocative, and it probably is, but it is meant to help us think through a trend that must be addressed in the life of the Christian church. Please think, before you react, and have dialogue with others about these points. I am seeking to address overall trends within the larger Christian community, and there are sure to be exceptions in various local congregations. If your church is an exception to the overall trend, then be thankful.

Pastor and Theologian

As congregations grew in total attendance in America throughout the Twentieth Century, church staff positions grew to meet the challenge of administrating the greater number of people, programs, and larger facilities inherent in this type of growth. Part of this pattern was for pastors to bring musicians to the staff who would take care of the musical aspects of worship and the ministry at large. Admittedly, pastors with large congregations have many responsibilities, and many pastors in fact have little musical ability to draw from. Thus, the addition of music staff only makes sense.

It seems, however, that as pastors continued to get busier and busier that they began to not only rely on the musicians for the musical leadership of worship, but also—in many ways—the spiritual leadership of worship. Rather than retaining an overall spiritual leadership as the pastor and leader of the congregation, they had to begin sharing this responsibility with others due to the overwhelming size and complexities of these ministries.

This is not necessarily a bad thing. I do not doubt that many gifted musicians are spiritually fit to lead a congregation in corporate worship. My question would be whether or not that is their appropriate place or responsibility, given the preparation they have received to fulfill this kind of role. When you begin to unfold the broadened understanding for a life of worship I have outlined in Parts I and II of this book, and by implication the broadened aspects of a balanced approach to corporate worship such as I have outlined in Part III of this book, one must realize the great load of responsibility that lies on the shoulders of what many churches simply call their "worship leader."

To get straight to the point, I would call for a re-evaluation of the kinds of requirements placed upon a candidate and eventual staff person who might fulfill this role of worship leader. Whether the trend began this way or not, what has become of this position is something that more noticeably resembles the role of a pastor than anything else. Call the position Associate Pastor, Worship Pastor, Pastor of Worship Arts, or whatever—but call it what it is. It is much, much more than leading music, and I think you could ask anyone who has filled this role to verify that.

This being the case, what must also come along with the title is the expectation of the preparation as a pastor. I think what is called for is Bible College, seminary, or some kind of higher education that focuses on Scripture, theology, and pastoral education. Many of those filling these roles have plenty of experience in order to lead music, but what I have discovered over and over is that they sorely lack the skills to function as a pastor to the people they are seeking to lead.

Rather than seeking and learning pastoral skills and training, there seems to be a plethora of opportunities to learn the "skills" of worship leading. In reviewing the class schedule of various of seminars, camps, and even college/university degree programs, what is found is a very basic (i.e., short) review of Bible and Theology, in contrast to a long, long list of music classes, as well as the modern aspects of multimedia (sound, lighting, computer, recording, video, etc.). The result is people better trained for jobs in Hollywood than for service in the church. In fact, I know of cases in which those trained with this emphasis have refused to attend or serve in churches that do not have the latest technological gadgetry.

What I find most puzzling is that churches (again, I am referring to what I see as overall trends that may not be true in all cases) accept this as what is needed. ***This is the kind of non-pastoral training for the person who has***

almost as much time to address and lead the congregation as the pastor—and sometimes even more! Do you find that strange? I could theorize about the reasons for this based upon some analysis of cultural influence on the church, but I think it is enough here to point out the situation and say, "Hey, wait, do you see what is happening here?!"

The position of worship leader is one that is first of all spiritual and pastoral. This must be established as the central focus and those filling these positions must be aware of what that means, as should the churches that hire them and the colleges, universities, and seminaries that train them. This means that the requirements placed on spiritual leaders in the pastoral Epistles (1 Timothy 3:1-13; Titus 1:5-9) will also be expected of the worship leader. Impeccable character, the ability to lead with spiritual wisdom, and the knowledge of doctrine and theology to refute error are the hallmarks of the elder, pastor, and deacon—as well as any spiritual leader of the church.

The Role of Pastor/Elder

In the New Testament there are many verses and comments that refer to the leadership of the people of God. The church is a living organism that relies on men of godly character to lead it and prayerfully follow its Head, Jesus Christ. Maybe this will be the outline for a future book, but I feel strongly enough about this gap in qualified leadership in the church that I would at least like to give a short outline for consideration and further study.

As the spiritual leader of the local church, the pastor and the worship leader must demonstrate the proper character as described by Paul in his letters to Timothy and Titus. Beyond these character traits, there are various responsibilities this individual is accountable for in his leadership of the church. The following five points is a broad representation of what those responsibilities include. Note that many of these references are directive in that someone is told what the role is, whereas others are observations about what someone is doing, or how Paul is treating those under his care. This list is not meant to be exhaustive, nor is it in order of importance, but these points clearly indicate important aspects of the pastoral role. If the worship leader holds a pastoral role, as I believe he does, then these criteria are for that person as well.

Responsibility #1 – *To teach, admonish, exhort, speak, defend, preach, strengthen, encourage, reason, persuade, debate, correct, demonstrate, steward, answer, call, proclaim, warn, equip, confirm, instruct, prescribe, reprove and rebuke.*

This responsibility is most often in reference to the word of God and doctrine (knowledge). It also pertains to teaching about how believers should live (lifestyle), based upon the word of God and doctrine. The best representation of the overall effect of this teaching role is Ephesians 4:11-16, where the following process is seen twice. The pastors and other leaders of the church are responsible: a) to equip the saints for service (proper working of giftedness); b) which leads to growth (building up in quality and quantity, unity and maturity); and c) results in the outward display of love!

Representative passages:
- Acts 5:42; 6:1-6; 8:28-29; 11:1-18; 13:5; 14:22; 15:1-2, 35; 16:46; 17; 18:5; 18:24-19:7; 19:8; 20:2; 22:1-28:28
- Romans 6:19; 7:21; 12:1-21
- 1 Corinthians 1:10; 2:1-5, 6-16; 3:1ff; 4:1; 5:1ff; 7:1ff; 11:23-24; 12:1ff; 15:1ff, 50ff; 16:13

- 2 Corinthians 1:6
- Galatians 1:6-9; 3:1ff; 6:10
- Ephesians 1:2; 4:1-16
- Philippians 1:5ff, 27; 2:1ff; 4:1, 14-20
- Colossians 1:7, 25, 28-29; 2:8; 3:18-4:1ff
- 1 Thessalonians 2:2, 13; 5:12
- 1 Timothy 1:3; 4:6, 11, 13
- 2 Timothy 2:2, 15, 22; 4:2
- Titus 2:1, 15

Responsibility #2 – *Attention to the pastor's own personal lifestyle and development*

The pastor is the servant of Christ (called by God), and steward of the church ministry (not a slave of the "church"). He is to be passionate, determined and disciplined for godliness and an example in all facets of life. At times he must defend himself, his actions and the church he represents, or other ministers of the gospel.

The pastor is to be caring, gentle and loving. He is to persevere in hardship, in the face of criticism, and through difficulties. Interestingly, he is to pay attention to his own gifts, development and spiritual life. Phrases such as *"pursue righteousness, godliness, faith, love, perseverance, gentleness"* or *"keep the gift with you fresh, and guard the treasure entrusted to you"* are evidence of this, along with a need for self-analysis. (See 1 Timothy 4:14-16; 6:11-20; 2 Timothy 1:6-14)

The pastor will also, at times, need to take care of himself (and others) financially, and so must have some valuable method of income beyond the church itself available to him. Paul models this aspect of ministry in his tent-making, which was apparently a quite lucrative occupation in the First Century. In Acts 18 there is evidence that he was able to support himself and others by "hopping" in and out of the business as needed.

Representative passages:
- Acts 18:1-5; 21:10-14
- Romans 1:1; 9:3; 13:1-7
- 1 Corinthians 4:1, 9-13; 9:3-18, 19-22
- 2 Corinthians 1:12; 4:7; 11:1ff
- Galatians 1:1; 1:11-2:10
- Philippians 1:1
- 1 Thessalonians 1:6; 2:4,7,9; 5:12 / 2 Thessalonians 3:7-10
- 1 Timothy 4:7, 12, 14-16; 6:11-20
- 2 Timothy 1:6, 14; 2:15, 22: 4:5

Responsibility #3 – *To work with church leadership*

This responsibility is to work with those in his flock. Scripture seems to indicate that pastors are responsible for the appointment of elders and deacons (Titus 1:5). It may be implied that pastors do this in consultation with other leaders (Acts 6), but it appears to be an appointment process rather than one of democratic election. Dismissal is the reverse of this and also his responsibility. He is also to teach elders and deacons.

The pastor is to provide guidance for worship and other church proceedings and to make use of fellow workers. He is to help the local body understand the need for financial support of the church, other churches, missions, and for the poor. He is responsible for strategy and planning for the ministry of the church as well.

The pastor will, at times, work with leaders of other churches. In regards to other pastors, he will sometimes instruct, rebuke, investigate, support, defend, dismiss, encourage, and confront them.

Representative passages:
- Acts 1:15; 4:35; 6:1-6; 8:14-17,26-27; 10:48; 11:22-29; 13:1-3, 51; 14:23; 15:13-22, 36; 20:17-35
- Romans 1:13; 14:1ff; 15:1ff, 25-28; 16:1ff
- 1 Corinthians 14; 16:1-4, 16 / 2 Corinthians 8-9
- Galatians 2:11-21
- Ephesians 6:21-22
- Philippians 1:1; 2:19-20
- Colossians 3:16
- 1 Thessalonians 3:2-3
- 1 Timothy 1:20; 3:1-13 / 2 Timothy 2:2
- Titus 1:5; 3:12-14

Responsibility #4 – *Prayer*

The fact that this responsibility is the underlying principle of everything else that the pastor does is undeniable. He is to pray for others, with others, as well as lead them in prayer and teach them how to pray. If we learn anything from this, it is that we do not pray enough.

Representative passages (only a small representation):
- Acts 1:14; 3:1; 4:23-31; 6:1-6; 13:1-3; 14:23; 20:36
- Romans 1:8
- 1 Corinthians 1:4 / 2 Corinthians 1:3
- Ephesians 1:15-21
- Philippians 1:5, 9-11
- Colossians 1:9-12
- 1 Thessalonians 1:2 / 2 Thessalonians 1:11
- 1 Timothy 2:1 / 2 Timothy 1:3

Responsibility #5 – *Giving perspective*

Keeping things in perspective for those he leads, the pastor is responsible to "keep the main thing the main thing." Some of the various areas he must keep in perspective are: attitude, suffering, hope, focus on Christ, God and man in relationship, history, the Christian life, and the circumstances of life.

Representative passages:
- Acts 16:24-25
- Romans 8:21-39
- 1 Corinthians 1:18-31
- 2 Corinthians 3:5; 5:11ff
- Galatians 3:1ff; 5:1ff
- Ephesians 1:3-2:10; 2:11ff; 5:1-6:24
- Philippians 4:10

Leadership of the church, the Body of Christ, is a high calling. We must be more diligent in seeking out competent, trained, faithful and spiritual men to lead our congregations. To do otherwise leads us to mediocrity and uselessness. As a person in a pastoral role, these things apply to the worship leader as well.

The Use of Music to Teach and Admonish

The general guidelines for the use of music in Colossians 3:16 also fall under the responsibility of the worship leader. We have discussed them previously, but now consider them within this context: *"Let the word of Christ richly dwell within you* [i.e., the corporate gathering], *with all wisdom teaching and admonishing one another with psalms and*

hymns and spiritual songs, singing with thankfulness in your hearts to God."
Note that there are basically two purposes in this verse for the word to dwell within the community: *teaching and admonishing.* The avenue, or vehicle, to carry teaching and admonishing is the music, specifically singing. Which is more important, the purpose or the vehicle? I would say they are both important in varying degrees. My point here is not to argue the importance of music, but to show that *teaching* and *admonishing* are pastoral duties. So whoever is doing this within the community must be equipped to do so—as a pastor to teach and admonish, and as a musician to do it through music. You can see the balance in this Colossians passage, but we can observe a lack of balance in many churches today.

We can also look to Ephesians 4:11-12 to underscore this point, and draw it together even tighter: *"And He gave some as apostles, some as prophets, and some as evangelists, and some as pastor-teachers,[53] for the equipping of the saints for the work of service..."* Colossians indicates the teaching duty of the worship leader, and here we see that the role of teacher and pastor are wrapped up in the same person in the local church. Bring all of this together, and the worship leader, by default, becomes a major spiritual leader within the local Body of Christ. Again, I bring these thoughts together to indicate the necessity of having people in that role that are qualified both as pastors and musicians.

For the worship leader/musician reading this it seems like a lot of work. What I seem to be saying is that someone called to be a worship leader must not only hone his or her skills as a musician, but also become educated in the same way as a pastor. Well, yes, that is exactly what I am saying. The worship leader is to be a pastor-musician. This is a dual role requiring parallel and complementary fields of study.

Some might think that I am way off base in suggesting this, however we can look at some of the most significant accomplishments in regards to music in the history of the church and see that the most influential of musicians have been well grounded Biblically and theologically. Such people as John and Charles Wesley, Isaac Watts, and John Newton are examples in recent centuries. Even further back we see the influence of Martin Luther and J.S. Bach. And beyond that even further, St. Francis of Assisi, or St. John Chrysostom and Ambrose were among church leaders that were both theologians and musicians. There are many more, and what we can find evident in those men, that we seldom find today, is a balance of theology and music in which the music is the vehicle for sound teaching and admonishment such as described in Colossians 3:16.

Musician

I must also address the other "half" of the picture. Just as I would call for a solid Biblical and theological education to prepare the worship leader to pastor the flock, I would also call for solid talent, education, and preparation to lead musically. The worship leader must be a *musician* as well.

If musicians who are filling worship leader roles felt picked on in the previous section, they might feel a little better once they realize that I will be picking on pastors and theologians in this section. Raise your hand if you are a musician that has ever been told by a pastor how to lead a song, what the tempo should be, how loud or soft to sing, what should happen with the "mix," who would make a "great" soloist or band member, or any other suggestion, request, or mandate that infers their expertise on the subject—when, in fact, they demonstrate weekly (or weakly!) that they have little musical expertise at all.

This is a baffling phenomenon that occurs regularly, and may have to do with the release of responsibility in which pastors have given a significant spiritual leadership role to the worship leader. Remember at the beginning of this chapter when I suggested that as congregations grew, pastors gave away spiritual leadership? Could it be that there is a subconscious desire to regain that leadership through the misguided suggestions, comments and observations that they make? I know this is just conjecture, but it would be an interesting study to pursue.

Nonetheless, I believe that pastors, having given them spiritual authority, should allow worship leaders the latitude needed to serve the church in this role. As a pastor-musician, there is a certain sense in which the worship leader will have a broader perspective on the Worship Service itself than the pastor does, unless that pastor is an equally talented musician.

You see, in the same way that it is inappropriate for a worship leader to be unbalanced by having a limited understanding of theology, it is just as inappropriate for a pastor who has little, or limited, musical ability and experience to be unbalanced. Although many pastors and theologians have written and taught about corporate worship and music, I must say that I find their presentations lacking when they admittedly lack the musical "chops" to speak intelligently about music and the disciplines of musicianship.

Music, by the very nature of what it is, is more than a talent. Music is a discipline and a craft. It is an art requiring both talent and skill. There may be a few musicians out there who have never needed a lesson and seldom practice, but the huge majority spend hours learning and practicing the craft and art of making music. It takes discipline, and when someone has "paid the price" of years and years of practice and performance, they deserve the credit for a certain expertise in that area. This means that pastors and their boards must give credit where credit is due and allow musicians to do the music. This is not a game to a musician, and the idea that we should let anyone and everyone on stage as part of a worship team is really "loony." Experienced musicians place high demands on themselves, and I believe there should be a certain expectation of skill for those joining in the leadership of worship. The fact that music is a discipline and a craft means that there may be times when someone has to be told that they are not welcome to perform or participate musically because they do not possess the required skill level to do so. I understand the need to help people with their self-concept, but this is not the right solution.

Of course, there should also be places for those who have basic levels of musical skills to serve the church and work to improve their abilities. Entry-level groups can be formed to rehearse basic repertoire and perform it as a "special" during a service. When the congregation knows that it is a teen group, children's group, or entry-level adult group there will be an appreciation of the effort without expectation of the highest quality. This really is OK. Not everyone is really good at performing, and everyone knows that.

And on another related point, let us call a spade, "a spade," when a musician performs. Whether it is a solo or with a group, it is a **performance**. They are **performing**, and we call it a **performance**. The fact that ministry or something special **might** happen does not legitimize renaming what they do. It seems somewhat subversive to me to hide these performances behind titles like: "Ministry in Music" or "Special Music" or "Ministry Performance." What happens if the elusive **ministry** does not actually happen, or the performance is **less than special**? We are not fooling anyone with these disguised titles, so we should avoid them.

The Dilemma

So we have a dilemma: on the one hand, there is a lot of talk out there (books, magazines, blogs, etc.) from worship leaders who are primarily musicians and have only a cursory, or layman's understanding of theology. On the other hand, there are those pastors and theologians talking out there (in books, magazines, blogs, etc.) who claim Biblical authority for their views but have no significant musical talent. The dilemma is that both of these perspectives are lopsided and unbalanced, and often the one "side" misrepresents and misunderstands the other "side."

Where are the leaders who desire significant study of Scripture and theology while at the same time are pursuing excellence in their musical craft? When will they write the books, teach the seminars, and establish the dialogue for corporate worship? I realize there are some able to speak in this arena, and are working diligently to educate pastors, musicians, and Christians in general regarding the full spectrum of worship. We must all face the reality, however, that by and large the dialogue, discussion, and agenda is actually established by musicians—specifically the ones with the top-selling CD's. I am not convinced that they should be the ones to do so.

Finally

In conclusion, my thoughts in this book are in pursuit of a filling a gap in the Twenty-first Century church that I identified over twenty years ago. The gap is in finding a solid presentation of what we have identified as "worship" and dealing with all of the Biblical, theological, and musical aspects of what that means, and what it looks like in real life.

I have found bits and pieces of this in the last twenty years, but no presentation that brings it all together such as I have attempted to do in these pages.

I have tried to present a Biblical model—a framework—that could under gird the most complex contemporary setting of life and worship in the big city, as well as the small intimate home church or church found in the local neighborhood. The concept of worship is one that must be considered integral to our entire life—as we live as individuals and in corporate gatherings.

Our theology of worship and the thoughts that drive our methods of worship must be clearly defined and communicated. These *internal* beliefs about worship will shape the *external* practice of worship. If the foundation is weak, so will the whole structure be weak.

Our study showed that the life of worship is broad. It began with a solid foundation of Biblical teaching about worship, which showed us the reality of worship as a lifestyle. The life of worship encompasses all that we do, being demonstrated in a life of love and service.

We then discovered how this life of worship extended into the expression of worship by the corporate body—in all of its fullness, diversity, and variety. The Church, the Body of Christ, serves the world out of the reality of each member living a life of worship on a daily basis. Worship, we found, is a totally integrated concept that flows into every area of individual and corporate life.

I hope this is a valuable addition to the studies on worship that have come before, and a spur to further discussion and consideration in the future. If nothing else, I hope that it has caused you to think more deeply and clearly about living a life of love and service—a true life of worship.

Appendix A: Recommendations for Further Study

I would recommend the following sources for further study. Although one can find a lot of information on the Internet, not all of it is worth the cyberspace it occupies. The authors I recommend below have proven track records and are quite qualified in the areas in which they write. If you have trouble locating any of these titles because they are out of print, check on www.amazon.com for new and used books, or www.used.adall.com for used titles.

On the Christian Life

- Martin Luther's *Small Catechism* and *Large Catechism* are excellent sources of foundational Christian teaching. Luther developed these specifically for use in the home with families and children. Available in various editions and translations.
- Luther's booklet called *The Freedom of the Christian* or *Christian Liberty* is another foundational writing helping the Christian to understand how their life fits into God's world. Available in various editions and translations.
- *True Spirituality* by Francis A. Schaeffer (Tyndale House Publishers, June 1979) gives a broad and thoughtful perspective on the true factors of the spiritual life of the believer.
- *Keys to the Deeper Life* by A.W. Tozer (Grand Rapids, MI: Zondervan Publishing House, 1973) is a short treatment with deep implications.

- *The Normal Christian Life* by Watchman Nee (Tyndale House Publishers, June 1977) is a classic on the topic.
- Other authors to look for: A.W. Tozer, C.S. Lewis.

On Worship

- *For All God's Worth: True Worship and the Calling of the Church* by N. T. Wright (Wm. B. Eerdmans Publishing Company, June 1997) is a series of sermons dealing with worship philosophy and practice.
- *The Dynamics of Corporate Worship (Ministry Dynamics for a New Century)* by Vernon M. Whaley (Baker Books, February 2001) is one of the better treatments of the many different elements of corporate worship.
- *Whatever Happened to Worship?* By A.W. Tozer (Camp Hill, Penn.: Christian Publications, 1985) is a classic mid-twentieth century call to appropriate thinking about worship.
- Other Authors: Look for anything by Robert Webber for excellent resources and thought over the last 30 years.

Worldview

- *Heaven is a Place on Earth* by Michael E. Wittmer (Zondervan Publishing House, 2004) is a primer on the subject of worldview.
- *Total Truth: Liberating Christianity from Its Cultural Captivity* by Nancy R. Pearcey (Crossway Books, June 2004) is an in-depth study and challenge to Western Christians (especially American

Evangelicals) to conform their worldview to Scripture.

- *The Complete Works of Francis A. Schaeffer: A Christian Worldview* (Crossway Books, 1982) would be one of the most complete studies of Christian Worldview and worth the purchase of all five volumes.

On Spiritual Gifts

- C. Peter Wagner has developed a solid study called *Discover Your Spiritual Gifts* (Regal Books, March 2005). This goes well with his *Finding Your Spiritual Gifts* (Regal Books, July 1995), which is a questionnaire to help identify gifts. Wagner has written several other studies as well, and is a leading authority in this area.
- *What's So Spiritual about Your Gifts* (Multnomah Publishers, April 2004) from Henry T. Blackaby and Melvin D. Blackaby also includes a book and study guide.

MBTI (Meyer-Briggs Temperament Indicator)

- *Please Understand Me II: Temperament, Character, Intelligence* by David Keirsey (Prometheus Nemesis Book Company, May 1998) is an outstanding guide to understanding personality.
- In regards to personality testing, I would also recommend finding someone in your church or another local church that has been through the training and certification to administer the MBTI. This will ensure the validity and proper interpretation of the results.

There are many, many other books and studies available on these subjects by other authors. I have only listed a few that I personally recommend and trust. When studying and pursuing further development in any way, it is always good to check with your pastor, or other well-read Christian leader. They will be able to recommend the best of resources for you, and help you avoid those that are less than adequate.

Appendix B: Creeds

I am including the text of the following Creeds as sources for basic Christian doctrine and foundational to a Christian worldview and belief system. These three are the most universal of all Creeds. Other Creeds generally veer off into denominational distinctives and are therefore not universally accepted. You will find good information about Creeds at www.creeds.net as well as www.ccel.org.

The Apostles' Creed

I believe in God the Father Almighty,
Creator of heaven and earth.

And in Jesus Christ his only Son our Lord;
who was conceived by the Holy Spirit,
born of the Virgin Mary,
suffered under Pontius Pilate,
was crucified, dead, and buried;
he descended into hell;
the third day he rose again from the dead;
he ascended into heaven,
and sits at the right hand of God the Father Almighty;
from there he shall come to judge the living and the dead.

I believe in the Holy Spirit;
the holy catholic Church;
the communion of saints;
the forgiveness of sins;
the resurrection of the body;
and the life everlasting. Amen.

The Nicene Creed

(A.D. 381, also known as the *Constantinopolitan Creed* or *Creed of 150 Fathers*)

We believe in one God,
the Father, the Almighty,
maker of heaven and earth,
of all that is, seen and unseen.

We believe in one Lord, Jesus Christ,
the only Son of God,
eternally begotten of the Father,
God from God, Light from Light,
true God from true God,
begotten, not made,
of one Being with the Father.
Through him all things were made.
For us and for our salvation
he came down from heaven:
by the power of the Holy Spirit
he became incarnate from the Virgin Mary,
and was made man.
For our sake he was crucified under Pontius Pilate;
he suffered death and was buried.
On the third day he rose again
in accordance with the Scriptures;
he ascended into heaven
and is seated at the right hand of the Father.
He will come again in glory to judge the living and the dead,
and his kingdom will have no end.

We believe in the Holy Spirit, the Lord, the giver of life,
who proceeds from the Father and the Son.
With the Father and the Son he is worshiped and glorified.

He has spoken through the Prophets.
We believe in one holy catholic and apostolic Church.
We acknowledge one baptism for the forgiveness of sins.
We look for the resurrection of the dead,
and the life of the world to come. Amen.

The Athanasian Creed

(mid-5th Century)

Whosoever will be saved, before all things it is necessary that he hold the Catholic Faith. Which Faith except everyone do keep whole and undefiled, without doubt he shall perish everlastingly.

And the Catholic Faith is this, that we worship one God in Trinity and Trinity in Unity.   Neither confounding the Persons, nor dividing the Substance. For there is one Person of the Father, another of the Son, and another of the Holy Ghost. But the Godhead of the Father, of the Son and of the Holy Ghost is all One, the Glory Equal, the Majesty Co-Eternal.

Such as the Father is, such is the Son, and such is the Holy Ghost. The Father Uncreate, the Son Uncreate, and the Holy Ghost Uncreate.   The Father Incomprehensible, the Son Incomprehensible, and the Holy Ghost Incomprehensible. The Father Eternal, the Son Eternal, and the Holy Ghost Eternal and yet they are not Three Eternals but One Eternal. As also there are not Three Uncreated, nor Three Incomprehensibles, but One Uncreated, and One Uncomprehensible. So likewise the Father is Almighty, the Son Almighty, and the Holy Ghost Almighty. And yet they are not Three Almighties but One Almighty.

So the Father is God, the Son is God, and the Holy Ghost is God. And yet they are not Three Gods, but One God. So likewise the Father is Lord, the Son Lord, and the Holy Ghost Lord. And yet not Three Lords but One Lord. For, like as we are compelled by the Christian verity to acknowledge every Person by Himself to be God and Lord, so are we forbidden by the Catholic Religion to say, there be Three Gods or Three Lords.

The Father is made of none, neither created, nor begotten. The Son is of the Father alone; not made, nor created, but begotten. The Holy Ghost is of the Father, and of the Son neither made, nor created, nor begotten, but proceeding. So there is One Father, not Three Fathers; one Son, not Three Sons; One Holy Ghost, not Three Holy Ghosts. And in this Trinity none is afore or after Other, None is greater or less than Another, but the whole Three Persons are Co-eternal together, and Co-equal. So that in all things, as is aforesaid, the Unity is Trinity, and the Trinity is Unity is to be worshipped. He therefore that will be saved, must thus think of the Trinity.

Furthermore, it is necessary to everlasting Salvation, that he also believe rightly the Incarnation of our Lord Jesus Christ. For the right Faith is, that we believe and confess, that our Lord Jesus Christ, the Son of God, is God and Man.

God, of the substance of the Father, begotten before the worlds; and Man, of the substance of His mother, born into the world. Perfect God and Perfect Man, of a reasonable Soul and human Flesh subsisting. Equal to the Father as touching His Godhead, and inferior to the Father as touching His Manhood.

Who, although He be God and Man, yet He is not two, but One Christ. One, not by conversion of the Godhead into Flesh, but by taking of the Manhood into God. One altogether, not by confusion of substance, but by Unity of Person. For as the reasonable soul and flesh is one Man, so God and Man is one Christ.

Who suffered for our salvation, descended into Hell, rose again the third day from the dead. He ascended into Heaven, He sitteth on the right hand of the Father, God Almighty, from whence he shall come to judge the quick and the dead. At whose coming all men shall rise again with their bodies, and shall give account for their own works. And they that have done good shall go into life everlasting, and they that have done evil into everlasting fire.

This is the Catholic Faith, which except a man believe faithfully and firmly, he cannot be saved.

End Notes

[1] For clarity, my own points of emphasis are in **bold italics**, and all Scripture quoted within the text will be found in regular *italics*.

[2] Michael E. Wittmer, *Heaven is a Place on Earth* (Grand Rapids, MI: Zondervan Publishing House, 2004), 21.

[3] Luther's work titled *On the Bondage of the Will* is part of the discussion, and a response to Erasmus' work titled *On the Freedom of the Will*. With this work Luther noted that Erasmus had "gone to the core" of the problem with Roman Catholic theology and practice.

[4] Roland H. Bainton, *Here I Stand: A Life of Martin Luther* (New York: The New American Library, 1950), 197.

[5] A.W. Tozer, *Keys to the Deeper Life* (Grand Rapids, MI: Zondervan Publishing House, 1973), 36-37.

[6] Horace E. Stoessel, "Notes on Romans 12:1-2" in *Interpretation* (Volume 17, Number 2), 161.

[7] Nancy R. Pearcey, *Total Truth: Liberating Christianity from Its Cultural Captivity* (Wheaton, IL: Crossway Books, 2004), 66.

[8] Stoessel, "Notes on Romans 12:1-2," 164.

[9] Francis Schaeffer, *True Spirituality* in The Complete Works of Francis A. Schaeffer: A Christian Worldview, Volume 3 (Westchester, IL: Crossway Books, 1982), 302.

[10] Stoessel, "Notes on Romans 12:1-2," 168.

[11] Stoessel, "Notes on Romans 12:1-2," 166.

[12] T.D. Jakes, *Intimacy with God: The Spiritual Worship of the Believer* in Six Pillars From Ephesians, Volume 3 (Tulsa, OK: Albury Publishing, 2000), 6.

[13] Ronald Allen and Gordon Borror, *Worship: Rediscovering the Missing Jewel* (Portland: Multnomah Press, 1982), 25-26.

[14] Augustine, *Confessions*, Trans. by Henry Chadwick (Oxford: Oxford University Press, 1998), 3.

[15] Paul Althaus, *The Theology of Martin Luther* (Philadelphia: Fortress Press, 1966), 251.

[16] Martin Luther, *Luther's Large Catechism*, Trans. by Dr. J.N. Lenker (Minneapolis: Augsburg Publishing House, 1935), 44.

[17] The idea of God's "Yes" in Christ in contrast to the "No" of sin and the Law is also a common theme in many theologians. It seems to me to be most highly definite in Martin Luther's writings in the contrast of Law and Gospel, as well as in Karl Barth's theology, the very nature of which is described in its name: Dialectic Theology.

[18] Vigen Guroian, "Seeing Worship as Ethics: An Orthodox Perspective" in *The Journal of Religious Ethics*, 334.

[19] See Luther's discussion of the First Commandment in his *Large Catechism*. Also reference Paul Althaus' chapter called "God's Will for Men" in his work *The Theology of Martin Luther* (Philadelphia: Fortress Press, 1966), 130-140.

[20] Josh McDowell, *The Last Christian Generation* (Holiday, FL: Green Key Books, 2006), 93.

[21] T.D. Jakes, *Intimacy with God,* 9-10.

[22] Pearcey, *Total Truth,* 153-247.

[23] Francis Schaeffer, *The God Who is There* in <u>The Complete Works of Francis A. Schaeffer: A Christian Worldview, Volume 1</u> (Westchester, IL: Crossway Books, 1982), 67.

[24] Pearcey, *Total Truth,* 48-49.

[25] Pearcey, *Total Truth,* 49.

[26] Martin Luther, "The Freedom of a Christian" in *Martin Luther's Basic Writings*, ed. by Timothy F. Lull (Minneapolis: Fortress Press, 1989), 617.

[27] Jeremy Begbie, "Music in God's Purposes" in *More Like the Master: A Christian Musician's Reader* (Chicago: Cornerstone Press, 1996), 108-109.

[28] For the full story read the history of Israel beginning in 1 Kings 11 through the book of 2 Kings. This history shows the willful disobedience of the Kings of Israel and Judah (with only a few exceptions), and the subsequent judgment of God and Israel's exile.

[29] John D. Witvliet, "The Spirituality of the Psalter: Metrical Psalms in Liturgy and Life in Calvin's Geneva," *Calvin Theological Journal*, 32 (November 1997), 282.

[30] E.E. Ryden, *The Story of Christian Hymnody* (Rock Island, IL: Augustana Press, 1959), 109.

[31] Charles Garside, *Zwingli and the Arts* (New Haven and London: Yale University Press, 1966), 45.

[32] Quoted by Garside, *Zwingli and the Arts*, 42.

[33] Geoffrey Wainright, *Doxology: The Praise of God in Worship, Doctrine, and Life – A Systematic Theology* (New York: Oxford University Press, 1980), 21.

[34] Wainright, *Doxology*, 21-22.

[35] Wainright, *Doxology*, 22.

[36] Wainright, *Doxology*, 22.

[37] A.W. Tozer, *Whatever Happened to Worship?* (Camp Hill, Penn.: Christian Publications, 1985), 44-45.

[38] This is an expansion of some principles presented by Ronald Allen and Gordon Borror, *Worship: Rediscovering the Missing Jewel* (Portland: Multnomah Press, 1982), 93-94.

[39] Wainright, *Doxology*, 242.

[40] Wainright, *Doxology*, 243.

[41] Francis Schaeffer, *Two Contents, Two Realities* in <u>The Complete Works of Francis A. Schaeffer: A Christian Worldview, Volume 3</u> (Westchester, IL: Crossway Books, 1982), 412.

[42] Begbie, "Music in God's Purposes," 129.

[43] Evelyn C. Schuette, "The Reformation and Musical Influences on Martin Luther's Early Protestant Hymody," *Reformed Liturgy and Music*, 16 (Summer 1982), 102.

[44] Martin Luther quoted by James F. Lambert, *Luther's Hymns* (Philadelphia: General Council Publication House, 1917), 15.

[45] Francis Schaeffer, *True Spirituality*, 300.

[46] Charles M Sheldon, *In His Steps* (Grand Rapids, MI: Chosen Books, 1984).

[47] Other passages that have a similar idea of balance include: 1 Peter 2:5-12 and 4:7-11; Hebrews 2:11-17; Philippians 3:3, 16-19; Ephesians 3:16-21 and 4:11-16; 2 Corinthians 8 and 9 (in regards to finances); and 1 Corinthians 6:17-20.

[48] Leon Morris, "Hebrews" in *The Expositor's Bible Commentary*, ed. by Frank E. Gaebelein (Grand Rapids: The Zondervan Corporation, 1981), 151.

[49] Guroian, "Seeing Worship as Ethics," 333.

[50] Allen and Borror, *Worship*, 39.

[51] By Christian Henry Bateman (1813-1899).

[52] By Brian Doerkson, © 1998 Vineyard Music.

[53] The text refers to "pastors and teachers," and I have chosen to render the translation according to what would help us in English identify this as not two separate roles filled by two separate people, but two functions of the same person in a local church. There is debate, yet many scholars understand this to be indicated in the Greek. A perusal of commentaries on this passage will find that this is the case.

Bibliography

Allen, Ronald and Gordon Borror. *Worship: Rediscovering the Missing Jewel.* Portland: Multnomah Press, 1982.

Althaus, Paul. *The Theology of Martin Luther.* Philadelphia: Fortress Press, 1966.

Augustine. *Confessions.* Trans. by Henry Chadwick. Oxford: Oxford University Press, 1998.

Bainton, Roland H. *Here I Stand, A Life of Martin Luther.* New York: The New American Library, 1950.

Begbie, Jeremy. "Music in God's Purposes." Pages 91-131 in *More Like the Master: A Christian Musician's Reader.* Chicago: Cornerstone Press, 1996.

Garside, Charles. *Zwingli and the Arts.* New Haven and London: Yale University Press, 1966.

Guroian, Vigen. "Seeing Worship as Ethics: An Orthodox Perspective." *The Journal of Religious Ethics,* 332-359.

Jakes, T.D. *Intimacy with God: The Spiritual Worship of the Believer* in <u>Six Pillars From Ephesians, Volume 3</u>. Tulsa, OK: Albury Publishing, 2000.

Lambert, James F. *Luther's Hymns.* Philadelphia: General Council Publication House, 1917.

Luther, Martin. *Martin Luther's Basic Writings,* ed. by Timothy F. Lull. Minneapolis: Fortress Press, 1989.

_____. *Luther's Large Catechism.* Trans. by Dr. J.N. Lenker. Minneapolis: Augsburg Publishing House, 1935.

McDowell, Josh. *The Last Christian Generation*. Holiday, FL: Green Key Books, 2006.

Morris, Leon. "Hebrews" in *The Expositor's Bible Commentary, Volume 12*, ed. by Frank E. Gaebelein. Grand Rapids: The Zondervan Corporation, 1981.

Pearcey, Nancy R. *Total Truth: Liberating Christianity from Its Cultural Captivity*. Wheaton, IL: Crossway Books, 2004.

Ryden, E.E. *The Story of Christian Hymnody*. Rock Island, IL: Augustana Press, 1959.

Schaeffer, Francis. *The God Who is There* in The Complete Works of Francis A. Schaeffer: A Christian Worldview, Volume 1. Westchester, IL: Crossway Books, 1982.

_____. *True Spirituality* in The Complete Works of Francis A. Schaeffer: A Christian Worldview, Volume 3. Westchester, IL: Crossway Books, 1982.

_____. *Two Contents, Two Realities* in The Complete Works of Francis A. Schaeffer: A Christian Worldview, Volume 3. Westchester, IL: Crossway Books, 1982.

Schuette, Evelyn C. "The Reformation and Musical Influences on Martin Luther's Early Protestant Hymody," *Reformed Liturgy and Music*, 16 (Summer 1982): 99-106.

Sheldon, Charles M. *In His Steps*. Grand Rapids, MI: Chosen Books, 1984.

Stoessel, Horace E. "Notes on Romans 12:1-2." *Interpretation*, Volume 17, Number 2: 161-175.

Tozer, A.W. *Keys to the Deeper Life*. Grand Rapids, MI: Zondervan Publishing House, 1973.

_____. *Whatever Happened to Worship?* Camp Hill, Penn.: Christian Publications, 1985.

Wainright, Geoffrey. *Doxology: The Praise of God in Worship, Doctrine, and Life – A Systematic Theology.* New York: Oxford University Press, 1980.

Wittmer, Michael E. *Heaven is a Place on Earth.* Grand Rapids, MI: Zondervan Publishing House, 2004.

Witvliet, John D. "The Spirituality of the Psalter: Metrical Psalms in Liturgy and Life in Calvin's Geneva." *Calvin Theological Journal,* 32 (November 1997): 273-297.

About the Author

Mark Sooy is a pastor, teacher, theologian, worship leader, and musician. His experience has led him through opportunities in pastoral church ministry, Bible college instruction, worship leading, authoring, conference speaking and leading, emergent church ministry, and other forms of Christian service.

Mark holds a Bachelor of Theology degree with an emphasis in Pastoral Studies from Grace Bible College (with a parallel major in music), as well as a Master of Arts in Historical Theology from Grand Rapids Theological Seminary of Cornerstone University. Both institutions are located in Grand Rapids, Michigan.

His other work includes articles for periodical publications, as well as the book *Essays on Martin Luther's Theology of Music*—which is a scholarly study of Luther's views on the arts, especially music, as it was formed and molded by his theology of creation. The study also compares Luther's thoughts with the other major Reformers.

Mark's wife, Elisabeth, often works alongside Mark in the various ministry opportunities that come their way. They currently reside in West Michigan with their three children: Estelle, Ashlea and Gordon.

For further information about Mark or Elisabeth and their ministries please visit: www.MarkSooy.com. You will find links to resources, a place to sign up for their e-Newsletter, and other information that may be of interest. You are also welcome to email Mark at mark@MarkSooy.com.

CPSIA information can be obtained
at www.ICGtesting.com
Printed in the USA
FFOW03n1010200118
44500664-44317FF